# THE CLINTONS

# AND THE

# GLASTONBURY CONNECTION

BLACKTHORN PUBLISHING

This book is written from the Heraldry, Coat-of-Arms
and Scrolls recorded in a rare early manuscript.
The provenance of the manuscript is certain
And is in private family ownership.

I am fully aware that I have an extraordinary book in my hands,
and that I must make the contents known.

Our early manuscript was featured with the author on the
world famous BBC Antiques Roadshow, recorded at
Cressing Temple Barns, Cressing, Essex, England,
where it was examined by, the much respected
Antiques Roadshow expert, Clive Farahar.

COPYRIGHT
All rights reserved; no part of this publication may be reproduced or transmitted by any means, electronic, mechanical, photocopied, recorded on any information storage or retrieval system without prior permission in writing from the publisher. ©2007


DISTRIBUTOR
Add Design
Britannia House
Bentwaters Business Park
Rendlesham
Suffolk IP12 2TW
United Kingdom
Telephone: (UK) 01394 460600
E-Mail: info@add-design.co.uk


ISBN 978-0-9557906-0-7


PUBLISHER
Blackthorn Publishing Ltd
Suite 404, Albany House
324-326, Regent Street,
London W1B 3HH
United Kingdom


Printers:
Colt Press Ltd, Unit 7C Perry Road, Witham Essex CM8 3UD UK

The author owes a debt of gratitude to his wife Sylvia Rayner, Lady of Annesley Grange, Nottinghamshire, for all the research and translation that made this book possible.

Special thanks also goes to Susan Thomas.

# AUTHORS NOTE and APOLOGY TO ORGANISED RELIGIONS

Part of the contents of this book reveals the unique history of the very first William Clinton in 1066 and the spread of the family name 'Clinton' to positions of high office in England and Ireland, following onto America.

Important amongst the Clinton line is the history of Bishop Roger Clinton, appointed Bishop of Coventry in 1137, at which time he was given custody of the 'Jesus Scroll'. The scroll that records where the Prophet Jesus spent his youthful years from the age of 14 to 28 years and how Jesus gained his remarkable and extraordinary abilities and powers in preparation for his ministry on return to Galilee

Leaders of world religions may not sit comfortably with new challenging historical information revealed in this book. However, the author would like to make it clear that there is no intention to be critical of any religious denomination or religious group. Nor of the romance about Jesus written into their own testaments over the centuries to gain both authority and appeal for their religion.

What is certain is that new information about the life of Jesus and the discoveries of the Knights Templar will continue to emerge from time to time. It may be that these discoveries will be at odds with the doctrine taught in the present days. However, it is the opinion of the author that whatever new information about the Prophet Jesus emerges from history will not make a jot of difference to the importance of the eternal truths taught by the Prophet Jesus. These are as relevant to leading a successful and fulfilling life in today's world, as they were when Jesus walked the earth.

# INDEX

|  | Page No. |
|---|---|
| Introduction | 1-5 |
| Prologue | 6-13 |
| Bishop Roger Clinton – 1137AD | 14 |
|     Roger Clinton | 15 |
|     The Jesus Scroll travels from Jerusalem to Kyiv. Ukraine | 15 |
|     Jesus – The Early Years | 16 |
|     Jesus and the Druids | 23 |
|     The sea of Spirit | 30 |
|     The return of Joseph of Arimethea to Cornwall from Galilee after the death of Jesus | 31 |
|     Blackthorn | 31-32 |
|     Jesus spoke of the Holy Spirit in a warning to Priests | 33 |
|     Sister Katarina's Miracle | 34 |
| Chamberlain of Normandy emerges as famous Knight William Clinton | 39 |
| Norman Knight William Clinton | 40 |
|     Knight William Clinton recruits Knights for the first Official Crusade | 43 |
|     William Clinton on a Personal Crusade to The Holy Land | 44 |
|     The Crusades | 47 |
|     The First Official Crusade 1096 – 1099 Led to the Capture of Jerusalem | 49 |
|     James the Brother of Jesus | 51 |
|     Gold and Documents uncovered in Jerusalem | 52 |
| Baron Clinton – Deputy Grand Master of the Knights Templar to King Edward 1 | 53 |
|     The Knights Templar vs. Baron John De Clinton | 54 |
|     The Rituals of the Order | 54 |
|     Remission of Earthly Sins | 54 |
|     Templars Onshore Tax Haven | 57 |
|     The Templar Wealth | 57 |
|     Cressing Templar Barn, Essex, England | 60 |
|     Cressing | 60 |
| Baron Clinton warns the French Templars of their impending Destruction. Gold tablets unearthed in Jerusalem sail for America leading to the birth of the Mormon Church | 65 |
|     The Templar Bank | 66 |

# INDEX

|  | Page No. |
|---|---|
| Friday The 13th | 66 |
| Mormon Church is indebted to Templar Knights | 67 |
| The Clintons led the Knights Templar to melt underground Into Freemasonry | 70 |
| The Knights Templar went underground but continued To be headed by Clintons | 71 |
| Development of Freemasonry | 72 |
| Modern Development in Freemasonry | 73 |
| Common descent of George Washington and William Spencer Churchill | 74 |
| The Clintons in Ireland - Irish love of America and Canada | 76 |
| Ireland | 77 |
| The Canadian Connection | 80 |
| The American Connection | 80 |
| Clintons in Ireland | 81 |
| Golden American Presidents and Generals with English Ancestors and their English Genes | 83 |
| General George Washington | 83 |
| Essex Wives for Sale | 86 |
| Background on Essex, England, the Garden of Eden | 87 |
| Essex Villages Prosper | 88 |
| The Bush family sail on the Mayflower | 88 |
| Essex Women and Craftsmen – The Best | 89 |
| The true story of Robin Hood – The dispossessed Earl of Huntingdon who changed the course of battlefield tactics Forever. | 90 |
| William Lord Clinton, Earl of Huntingdon, Lord Admiral Of England and Ireland succeeded to the title of Earl of Huntingdon | 90 |
| Robin Hood vs William Clinton – Earl of Huntingdon | 93 |
| Robin Hood | 93 |
| The Real Robin Hood | 94 |
| The Longbow | 96 |
| The Norman Sheriff of Nottingham | 116 |
| The Game of Noughts and Crosses | 118 |
| Knight Rayner the Flemming and Robin Hood | 118 |

# INDEX

| | Page No. |
|---|---|
| Archery Speed Contest | 119 |
| The Death of Robin Hood | 119 |
| The Potter's Tale | 123 |
| Topography | 125 |
| The Three Edwards 1272-1377 | 125 |
| Ancient Background History | 126 |
| A Personal View of the Battle of Hastings 1066 | 127 |
| Viking turned Norman -Duke William of Normandy, France | 130 |
| Duke William of Normandy | 131 |
| England's Edward the Confessor 1049-1065 | 134 |
| England's King Harold | 135 |
| Notes – Holy Relics | 136 |
| Duke William's Plan to become King of England | 137 |
| Viking Diversionary attack on York | 138 |
| The Vikings Win York | 139 |
| King Harold falls for William's planned diversion and Arrives in York to take on the Vikings | 140 |
| England's King Harold Recaptures York | 141 |
| While Harold was away, Duke William lands on England's South Coast | 144 |
| England's King Harold panics and returns South | 146 |
| King Harold foolish to take on Duke William | 147 |
| The Battle Begins | 147 |
| William's tactics wear down the English shield Wall | 148 |
| Duke William closes on Harold for the Kill | 148 |
| King Harold is Killed – Duke William is Victorious | 149 |
| English History Classes ignore French Domination and influence | 150 |
| England A Province of Normandy | 150 |
| King William moves to secure his Kingdom in England | 151 |
| English Bishops replaced by Normans | 152 |
| Doomsday Book | 152 |
| The Death of William The Conqueror | 153 |
| The Clintons Rise and Rise | 153 |
| The author's notes on 50 years of Religious Study | 161 |
| Stop Blaming God | 161 |
| Politics to Exclude Women from the Church as Priests and Teachers | 163 |
| Indisputable Precedents for Women Priests and Bishops | 164 |
| More Politics About James the Brother of Jesus | 165 |

BBC ANTIQUE ROADSHOW, HELD AT CRESSING TEMPLE BARNS, ESSEX, ENGLAND. AUTHOR RONALD RAYNER (LORD CARLTON LYNDRICK) CENTRE. CLIVE FARAHAR, BOOK EXPERT ON LEFT…"THE BOOK IS PRICELESS". GRANDDAUGHTER EMMA SELLEARS ON RIGHT

"This book is the most important attachment to history since the discovery of the Dead Sea Scrolls" *Sylvia Rayner*

# Introduction

Anyone who doubts that there is a connection through the loop of time in our local universe linking the past to the future and a feedback in the loop of time connecting the future to the present, should consider the events that unfold in this book.

If you have ever looked into a mirror in a moment of quiet and wondered whom it is staring back, the answer is deeper than you may think. The person you see in the mirror is only part of the story of the person staring back. There are hundreds of other generations of people who have contributed to the DNA and genes within the person reflected in the mirror. Distant relatives who you will certainly never meet and you may never ever learn of their existence, but exist they did, and they continue to live on in your genes.

Most people will know about the life of their parents or grand parents, or even their great grand parents, but what about the individuals before them; The distant relative who passed on their DNA to them and you. What was their place in their society? What did they have to do to survive in their lifetime, what was their story? Were they even living in the same country? Which part of their genes have you inherited? What inherited traits from your ancestors live on in you and are they genes to die for? If your name is Clinton, Bush or Washington, you certainly have inherited genes to die for!

DNA is a nucleic acid that is the main constituent of all organisms on the planet. DNA is self-replicating and plays a central role in the transmission of hereditary characteristics from parent to offspring. Your DNA records where you came from thousands of years in the past, and is your passport through time.

The structure of DNA molecules takes the form of a double helix – two strands coiled around each other. During replication the strands of the helix separate, producing identical copies of the original helix – accurate self-replication.

An expert working in a laboratory can extract DNA from bones and other body parts many thousands of years old with the qualification that the remains have been preserved in conditions that have enabled DNA to survive. Once extracted, DNA from ancient body parts (or body fluids) can be compared with the DNA of people living today. One of the uses of this information is to provide a pointer for people living today to where the area or region their ancestors originated.

Entanglements in time allow for the future to cast a shadow back to the present, and I know of no finer example of this than the future portended for Hillary Clinton. Hillary Clinton is destined, at some time in the future to become the first woman President of the United States of America.

There is a clear entanglement in time casting a shadow into the present by the actions of an English ancestor of America's Hillary Clinton, wife of former President Bill Clinton. A shadow portending Hillary Clinton's destiny; to become the first woman President of the United Sates of America at some time in its future. A shadow brought to life and highlighted by that great newspaper the U.K. Sunday Times. Here is the article written by Maurice Chittenden, and the photograph used that tells its own story. All by kind permission of my favourite newspaper, the Sunday Times, which I have read for 50 years come December 2007.

## AUTHORS RECOMMENDATION

It is vital for world economics that America remains in a safe pair of hands after any upcoming Presidential election in the USA.
Logic and common sense indicate that the safest pair of hands are those of Hillary Clinton. Added to which Hillary has the backing of her husband Bill Clinton, one of the most succesful and talented Presidents who sat in the White House

# When Hillary's English cousin took a Liberty

■ **Maurice Chittenden**

BORN to be president of the USA? Hillary Rodham Clinton may not have made it yet but one of her British cousins lit the way with her torch.

Emily Roddam, a distant relative of Clinton, dressed up as the Statue of Liberty in Co Durham in 1941 to celebrate America's war aid to Britain — and the Stars and Stripes may be flying there again if Clinton becomes the first elected female president.

Durham county council is almost certain to invite her to visit the area if she returns to the White House. The council previously invited her and her husband, President Bill Clinton, 10 years ago but they never came. If Air Force One does touch down at Durham Tees Valley airport, it will be Hillary's northern relatives who will be cheering the loudest.

Clinton could time the visit for 2011 to mark the 130th anniversary of her great-grandfather's departure to the United States. In 1881, at the age of 38, Jonathan Roddam, a colliery overseer who was descended from a family of miners in Co Durham, made his way to the coalfields of Scranton, Pennsylvania, in search of work and later became a policeman and a florist.

His own grandfather was called Jonathan Roddam — the two spellings of the surname were interchangeable at that time — who was born at Chester-le-Street in Co Durham in 1779.

It is from him that the woman who dressed up as the northeast's Statue of Liberty was descended. Emily, then 25, was also born in Chester-le-Street. She was working as a nanny for the Kidd family in Washington, then in Co Durham but now part of Tyne and Wear, when she put on her costume for a town parade to help to celebrate the American lend-lease programme to send war supplies to Britain.

Delena Kidd, the actress,

**Don't mess with Hillary**
page 25

and daughter of the town's GP at the time, said last week: "I was seven in 1941 and remember it very well. My mother organised the parade and Emily Roddam was a great attraction.

"It is such a coincidence because she must be related to Hillary. I can see the resemblance. She has the same jaw, the same lovely wide cheeks, rounded cheekbones and the same rather grand look."

There must be something in the water in the northeast: George Washington, the first US president, traced his family to Washington, then a village that stood on land once owned by the Bishop of Durham.

Emily Roddam dressed as the Statue of Liberty in 1941 to celebrate US war aid to Britain

What the inheritance in the DNA construction shows is that we are to a greater or lesser extent pre-programmed into the future, whilst at the same time remaining entangled in time past.

Science tells us that some inherited traits may jump one or two generations, but they will emerge to dominate at sometime in the future.

Enthusiasts with both the time and the know-how can trace their ancestry back a few centuries, but to know your family history in detail back through a thousand years and beyond, you would be that one lucky individual in countless millions.

If your surname is CLINTON then you are one of those lucky people in countless millions because this book is going to take you on a journey through time to the family from which you almost certainly descended, and the genes you inherited as far back as the year 1066.

If your name is Clinton, your DNA has travelled down through centuries to the present time through the ruling elite of England and Ireland, by courtesy of a Norman Knight who came to England with William the Conqueror in 1066.

If you are a descendant of a family named Bush, you also have genes to die for. It is probable that your ancestors were one of the most successful seed merchants and farmers in Southern England. Your ancestors were the first seed merchants to export commodities to the USA before the family itself emigrated to America, leaving forever their place of origin in Essex, England.

Another way of tracing the spread of a family from a single ancestor through to the present day is through the use of historic records. There is however severe limitations in most parts of the world in retrieving historic records reaching back say, 500 years or more and that is what makes this book so unique, because it is my contention that it was the English genes washing through the veins of these early American Presidents that were responsible for making America the great nation that it is today. When Hillary Clinton is elected President, her genes will give that lady the ability to make yet another great American President; every bit as capable as her husband Bill Clinton.

*Where would America be today without those English genes that made their leader successful and great?*

It flows back through nearly 1000 years entangling a trio of Golden American Presidents and on to the early years of Jesus from the age of fourteen years until he took up his ministry.

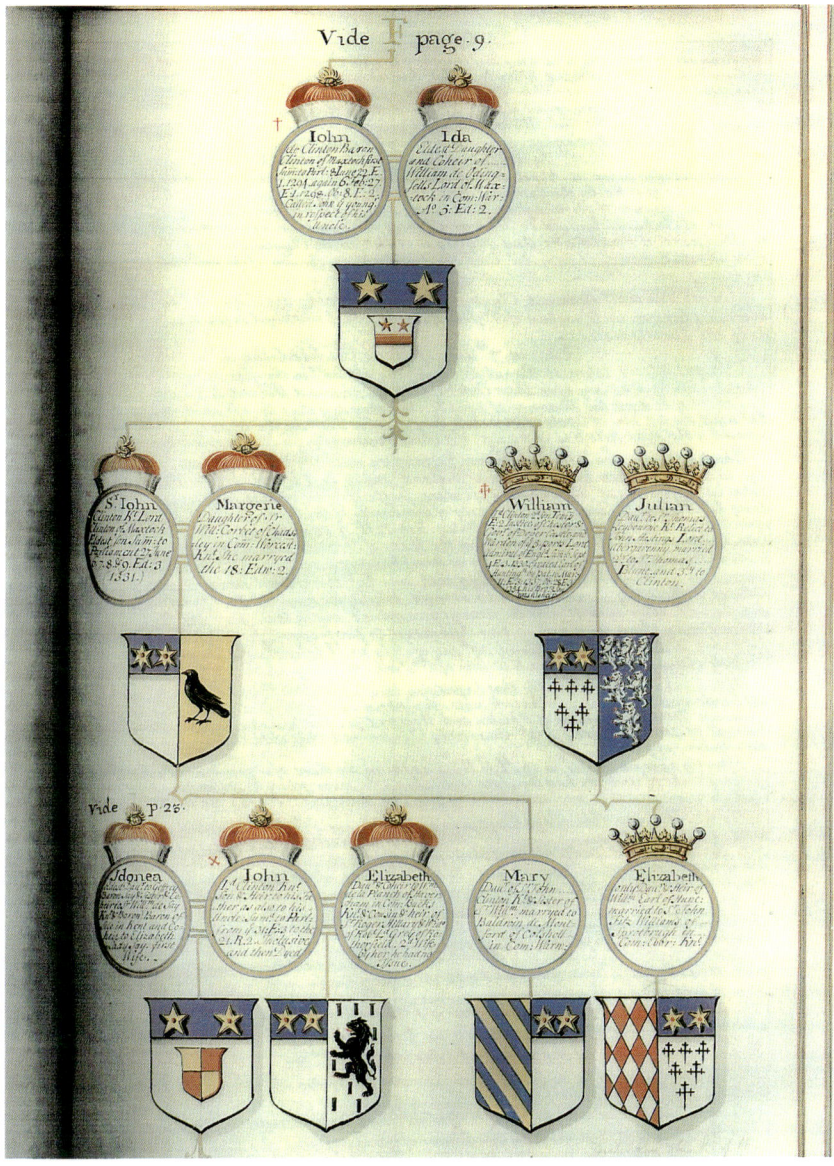

# Prologue

Our rare translation of what is known as 'The Jesus Scroll' travels back in time through two thousand years of English history to the age when Joseph of Arimathea brought Jesus and his own son (at the ages of fourteen years) to Cornwall in England. Boys became men in Jewish tradition at the age of fourteen years when they were sent to learn their trades. Cornwall was the only centre in the World at that time with both the raw materials and expertise to smelt metals and mine. These metals were highly prized by the Romans and sought after by traders in every part of the world.

Smelting ferrous and non-ferrous metals were traditions in Cornwall that reached back to the Bronze Age 3000 years before Joseph arrived. Jesus and his cousin were to remain on the already well-established Jewish community in Cornwall to learn and master the many trades practiced by the Anglo Saxons for centuries.

Our rare family owned book seen on the BBC Antique's Roadshow moves on a thousand years from the Jesus Scroll to a Chancellor of Normandy, France. A Knight who acquitted himself well in battle, a member of the Norman nobility who came to England and adopted a name from Oxford, England – the name of William Clinton.

Our Knight intermarried successfully and rose through to the top of the ruling classes of England; whose descendants become Dukes, Earls, Lords of Manors, Governors, Generals, and Admirals, one changing his name and going on to become a Prime Minister of England with another appointed Bishop of Coventry.

The Clintons also held important Governorship's in Ireland, plus a Generalship during the American War of Independence. Daughters of the Clintons were born in the Parish of St Peter, Dublin before moving with their husbands to America.

It is our opinion that the original Coat-of-Arms of the Clinton family gave rise to the design of the American flag: the great stars and stripes of America.

In 1157 Roger Clinton, Bishop of Coventry, ancestor to the first Bill Clinton, obtained a rare scroll uncovered by Templar Knights in Jerusalem that went to Kyiv Ukraine for translation by the Monks of the early Sophia Monastery. The translation records details of the early life of Jesus after he left Jerusalem with his wealthy uncle, Joseph of Arimathea at the age of fourteen years.

Moving on, the French King Louis Fourth decided to destroy the Orders of Knights Templar with two objectives in mind. The first and most important so far as the French King was concerned was to rid him of the repayment of the huge sums of money he owed to the Templars. Secondly and equally important was the prospect of stealing for himself all the land, properties and money belonging to the Templars to finance his extravagant life style.

Rome owed large sums of money to the Templars; debts built up during the Crusades from pledges made but never paid. Rome was also angered by the disloyalty of many Templars who had strayed beyond the control of Rome's Priests to follow their own religious services based on the contents of ancient scrolls. These first century scrolls taught believers that they could pray direct to God and did not require the intervention of a Priest for remission of their sins.

This was not a story Rome wanted to hear or a story to be repeated. Rome moved quickly to side with the French King and supported the destruction of all the Orders of Knights Templars in Europe, and the seizure of their property and goods.

Informants from the Templar branches in England gave many Templar groups in France time to collect their treasures and scrolls, and flee to other countries before their destruction. One group sailed for America with ancient gold tablets containing the writing from the days of the Old Testament. It is probable that these gold tablets were those uncovered by Joseph Smith, Founder of the Mormon Church in America. Many of the Templar groups went underground to emerge as the Order of Freemasons. Our book explains how the Masonic lodges formed from the eighteenth century onwards came down a very different route.

Glimpsing ahead to the other sections of the rare manuscripts, amazingly there is also a connection in our manuscript between the name Clinton, and the world famous tales of Robin Hood, and his merry men who lived in Sherwood Forest, Nottingham, England, and said to have robbed the rich to give to the poor. Robin Hood was the dispossessed Earl of Huntingdon, a position held later by William Lord Clinton, another descendent of the first Bill Clinton.

William Clinton was very successful on the battlefield at Hastings. Together with Rayner The Flemming, (the author's ancestor), who commanded the right flank of William the Conquerors' Cavalry at Hastings; the two fine knights led the charge that broke through King Harold's shield wall holding back the Normans from victory.

Roger Clinton was appointed Bishop of Coventry in 1137. The Clinton families endowed many Monasteries throughout England to house Monks, and Priories for Nuns, as did the author's ancestors Rayner the Flemming endowed the Priory at Kirklees where Robin Hood died. It was a popular belief in those times that the simpler the life of the religiose, the closer to God they would become and the more likely their prayers would be answered. The Clintons obviously wanted to be close to God and if their meteoric rise through the ranks of Dukes and Earls is any guide, the Clintons were very successful. The Clintons were also successful in following the King William's wishes that Norman Nobles should marry into the English ruling classes.

Amongst the many notable Clintons was Henry Feines Clinton, Earl of Lincoln, his Motto in his Coat of Arms is in ancient French – "Loyalty has no shame" proving the Norman ancestry. Earl Clinton became Duke of Newcastle under Lyne, when his cousin Thomas Pelham Holles died. King George allowed the Earl of Lincoln the Duke of Newcastle to change his name to Pelham, under which name he became Prime Minister of England (1743-1754). The Kings permission is recorded in our manuscript.

It is very obvious by the number of important posts held by the Clintons in Ireland, that the families were very fond of that country. Indeed, one Lord Clinton fought on the side of the Irish in the field against the English invaders.

English General Sir Henry Clinton, later Lord Clinton, based his command center in New York during the War of Independence in America. His adversary, General George Washington, is depicted in a beautiful stained glass window in the town of Maldon in the county of Essex, England, where the last English ancestor of General George Washington, his great, great Grandfather an English clergyman, is buried. That great Englishman Winston Churchill shares common ancestry with George Washington.

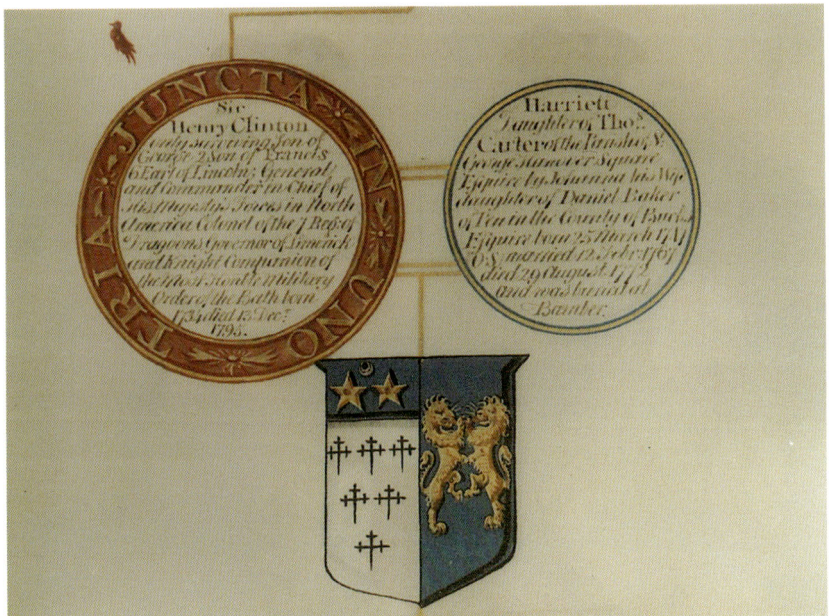

### AUTHOR'S NOTE:

The Knights Templar uncovered the Jesus scroll when they were building the steps down to the tomb of Holy Mary and laying the paving around the tomb in the heart of the old city of Jerusalem.

Henry Clinton, 7th Earl of Lincoln 1684-1728 and Thomas Pelham-Holles, 1st Duke of Newcastle 1693-1768. Painted by G. Kneller circa 1721

Extract from the Manuscript detailing the King's granting Lord Clinton, Duke of Newcastle, permission to use the Surname of Pelham.

Extracts from the Manuscript detailing Henry Clinton,
as the 7th Earl of Lincoln

The secrets contained in the Ancient first century scrolls of which the Knight William Clinton will have been aware, stayed in his family until the fifteenth century and beyond. Over those centuries the Clinton family (in England and Ireland) and their descendents became rich and powerful. Consorts of Kings and Princes, and Deputy Grand Masters of the Order of Knights Templar within Royal circles. Never ever abusing their wealth, power and position.

America's first President, General George Washington, had English genes running through his veins from the DNA passed on to him from his English ancestral ministers of the Church. How long would the fullness of that great nation have been delayed without English genes to set her on her course to become one of the most powerful and influential nations in the world? God bless America.

# BISHOP ROGER CLINTON.
## 1137AD

A DIRECT DESCENDANT OF THE FIRST WILLIAM CLINTON

The early life of Jesus recorded in an ancient scroll brought from Jerusalem by the Knights Templar and held by Bishop Roger Clinton, Bishop of Coventry, England in 1137.

Roger Clinton consecrated Bishop of Coventry – 1137

# Roger Clinton

Roger Clinton was elevated to the post of Bishop of Coventry and Custodian of the Jesus Scroll by King Henry I in 1137.

Crusader Knights William de Warren and Rayner the Flemming unearthed the Jesus Scroll, during the construction of what are widely known as the "Crusader Steps" leading down to what is said to be the tomb of Holy Mary in Jerusalem, where her remains were put to rest after being removed from the Kedron Valley. Queen Helena, Roman Empress, and Mother of Constantine the Great ordered the transfer. The tomb is beautiful with loving care lavished on the tomb itself; the floor around the tomb and the steps leading down to the tomb is obvious, even to the present day.

## The Jesus Scroll Travels from Jerusalem to Kyiv. Ukraine

The only place in the known world where mixed Asian and middle eastern language scrolls could be translated into a form understood by the Norman French were the Monasteries of Kyiv, Ukraine.

Our early history of that interesting city reveals that Viking raiders travelled down the rivers from Europe towards the Black Sea looking for a place to settle far away from the constant warring in their own lands. These Viking travellers were the true early founders and settlers of the cities of Kyiv and Novgorod. Rurik, a Norseman, became ruler of Kyiv in 850.

Not surprisingly, Crusaders with their Viking/Norman ancestry were always happy to travel to Ukraine where they would enjoy a warm reception from a people ruled over by a Christian Prince who supported the Crusader cause. Many in the local population were also aware of their own Viking roots.

In 988 AD Vladimir, Prince of Kyiv, had been baptised into Christianity. The Roman Emperor of Constantinople acted as his guide and Godfather. Vladimir set up a Monastery for Christian learning in the woods in Kyiv. The Crusaders exchanged the original scroll in payment for the translation, plus their shelter and accommodation at the monastery. The Knights set off on their return journey to England with their valuable scroll and to claim their reward from King Stephen. King Stephen gave the scroll to his trusted religious scholar Roger Clinton on his appointment by the King, to the important position of Bishop of Coventry.

## JESUS - THE EARLY YEARS

The translation of the Jesus Scroll reveals that the boy Jesus left Nazareth at the age of twelve years to accompany his wealthy uncle; much respected by the Romans, the Jewish trader and Rabbi Joseph of Arimathea, together with Joseph's youngest son who was around the same age as Jesus and called Adan.

The Scroll records that the Prophet Jesus was the Son of Joseph, a carpenter and smithy whose home and extended family were in Galilee. However, Joseph maintained a workshop in Nazareth because of its position on the very busy trade and caravan route to Sepphoris and beyond, a strategy that brought much business into Joseph's workshop. Jesus' three brothers and two sisters, all lived on a farm with their grandparents in Galilee. The grandparents headed an extended family of farmers spread throughout Galilee. All of the members of the family were devoutly religious, and were the driving force in setting up meeting houses in the villages throughout Galilee.

John the Baptist, the cousin of Jesus, headed the whole movement. Jesus, being the eldest son, stayed with Joseph and Mary in Nazareth both to help his father in the workshop whilst at the same time learning the trades for which the family were well known.

It was a happy time for Jesus, Joseph and Mary in Nazareth as they went about their daily business, but it was a happy way that was not to last. Troublesome Jewish zealots brought tragedy to the area almost overnight. Sepphoris, a town on a hill about 30 furlongs distant from Nazareth was set ablaze by the Roman Emperor, Herod Antipas, as a punishment for an abortive resurrection and attempt on his life by Jewish zealots.

Two thousand local inhabitants were rounded up and crucified as an example and warning to others. Nazareth was a small place, and there was no way to avoid seeing the corpses rotting on the crosses in the distance at every point on the compass by everyone going about their daily business.

Roman soldiers relentlessly pursued anyone opposed to Roman rule. Everyone faintly under suspicion was arrested, and executed without trial by crucifixion. Joseph and Mary were particularly afraid for their son Jesus, because he was not one to cower before the Roman oppressors. Joseph and Mary decided to take Jesus to the safety of Galilee, to the care of his wealthy uncle, Joseph of Arimathea who was influential in senior Roman circles. A member of the Sanhedrin family and a trader of all sought after commodities particularly metals. They begged Joseph to take Jesus from Palestine on his next trip to Europe and keep Jesus abroad with him until such a time that it was safe for Jesus to return to Galilee and Jerusalem.

In the course of his business Joseph travelled extensively to European Ports to barter silk, salt, spices and luxury goods from the Middle East. He would then sail on along the centuries old route to the West Coast of England to satisfy the Romans insatiable desire for metals.

The West coast of England was the golden gateway to the major World source at that time of ferrous and non-ferrous metal ores and metal ingots. These were all essential to the manufacture of Roman armour and weaponry.

Metals were amongst the most sought after by the Romans of all the World's commodities. It was the availability of copper, tin, lead, silver and iron that first drew the attention of the Romans to Britain's shores.

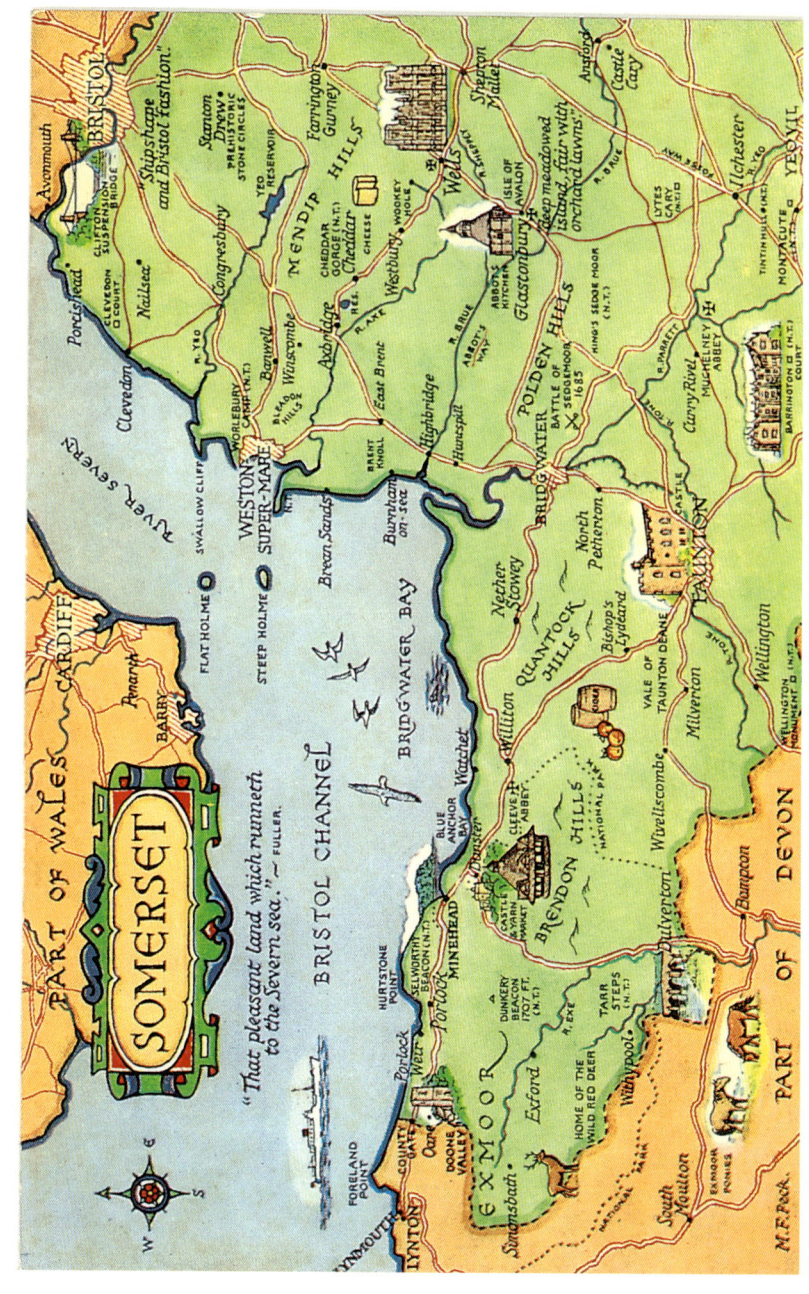

POSTCARD DATED 1907 - SOMERSET

18

However, long before the Romans arrived with their road building skills, the rivers in Cornwall and Somerset were ready made natural highways essential to the miners and smelters for the transportation of its heavy loads to trading points inland and to the costal ports.

Long flat-bottomed log boats hewn from a single tree were reliable in carrying a goodly load at a moderate pace to their destination. The long history of this system of transportation for moving metals along the rivers dates back thousands of years to the Bronze Age.

Not only were these small boats connected by the many rivers extending to the Cornish Coast, but routes also ran through to the North Channel in the West.

Pilton Harbour in Somerset became a main trading post to which the tinners, lead and silver makers, brought their ingots for weighing, barter and sale. Pilton was used extensively by Joseph of Arimathea and his team to assemble loads along the route from the Mendip Plateau down to the coast. At Pilton, ingots were stored in a small wattle and daub Meeting House built by Joseph and his band to accommodate the party during the sometimes, long wait through the Winter months.

Joseph arrived with his small crew, including the two trainees at Looe Island, which was around a mile wide on Britain's Cornish coast. They would unload the cargo from their ship into a wattle and daub hut on the island, which would be their storage centre for their stay. From there they would sail a much smaller boat into the Fowey, which was a major English port at the time. This disembarking was a necessary precaution for their safety. Fowey harbour was treacherous and strewn with obstacles during really heavy gale force storms. St. George's Island was also treacherous during storms. Fowey could boast double the number of ships entering the port compared to those sailing the Thames into London in those times.

## AUTHOR'S NOTE

The Mendip Plateau was 165 cubits high, a day's journey in length, and a quarter of a day in breadth. The plateau was situated close to a forest, which meant that the smelters had access to the wood required to enable their fires to reach the temperatures needed to make good pure metal blocks.

POSTCARD DATED 1905 GLASTONBURY ABBEY RECONSTRUCTED

Frequent surges from the sea to the north of Cornwall made it possible to sail along the rivers inland as far as Glastonbury Tor, which, at high tide, was surrounded, by water; on top of the Tor was a Druid Temple, and at certain times the water round this Tor shone as like a glass mirror, giving this Tor a magical look.

Joseph had many Jewish friends and relatives who owned most of the smelters along the rivers where tin was found. They were happy to trade their tin blocks in exchange for the various commodities and luxuries Joseph had brought with him from the Far East and Europe. Joseph also targeted other metals such as Copper, Lead and Silver from other smelters for barter in exchange for goods.

Joseph recorded the fact that Anglo Saxons were excellent miners. The men crawled deep into underground caves to retrieve malachite (copper), which they gouged from the walls with bone tools in the same way their ancestors had done for 3000 years. The malachite would be transported two hundred kilometres to the smelters to exchange for goods necessary for their livelihood. Lead, silver and iron ore were transported to Joseph from the Mendip Hills. Joseph was a key player in this circle of trade. Much trusted and respected for his knowledge, Joseph and his family grew very wealthy.

The following morning, ingots acquired by Joseph and his two young traders would be sailed back to Looe Island. Ballast from their ship would be unloaded, equal in weight to the ingots stowed on board. Great skill was needed in handling these small ships, which had neither compass charts nor maps. No attempt would be made to make a return journey to the Middle East in these ships during the winter months when ships could be easily lost along the treacherous Cornish Coast. Winter was a great time for the young apprentices Jesus, and his cousin. With time on their hands, they learnt much about the methods of catching the Cornish Herring; methods they could use on the lake back in Galilee. They were also taught how to extract oil from fish, a valuable commodity that could be stored in barrels. They also saw how the fishermen used the salt they had brought to Cornwall to preserve fish so that the fish would keep indefinitely. Oil and preserved fish were prized commodities that could be bartered at any European Port.

POSTCARD DATED 1905
GLASTONBURY ABBEY, ST. JOSEPH'S CHAPEL, ALTAR OF JOSEPH OF ARIMATHEA

Jesus and his cousin remained in Cornwall to continue business while Joseph returned with a fully laden ship via European ports to Israel. The young men were quite safe as Joseph was one of the few metal merchants authorised to use the Roman Imperial Stamp on ingots at the smelters. Everyone was aware that Jesus and his cousin could bring the much-feared Roman soldiers from the small Cornwall Garrison if they ran into any serious problems.

Joseph of Arimathea was well known and respected in the areas surrounding the smelters as an authority on the Jewish Law and he became a sought after speaker throughout the area. Joseph's travels gave Jesus and his cousin the opportunity to meet with all the tribal priests and leaders of the Druid communities and to study the practices and customs of their holy men. This included their methods for healing and casting out devils, which involved much ceremony, the daubing of blue paint (wode) and the ingredients and preparations of potions that could take away feeling and pain after a serious injury.

## JESUS AND THE DRUIDS

The local Druids regarded Joseph of Arimathea as an exulted teacher from a land far off, which they knew to be the land of the great prophets. The Chief Druid went to Joseph's camp, with the message that is was clear to the local Druid Priests that Joseph was also a man of their One God; a Prophet and teacher revered by your own people. You are a teacher to your student Jesus who shows undoubted unique and outstanding qualities for a youth of his age. Forever questioning the Druid Priests and Priestesses about their philosophy and teachings; acquainting them with the teachings of the Prophets in his own lands with knowledge far above his years. The Chief Druid invited Joseph to attend with his two students, a Druid Ceremony to be held on the following day, the day of the full moon, and before Sunset.

POSTCARD DATED 1905
GLASTONBURY. ST. MICHAEL'S TOWER

It was late in the afternoon when the trio arrived at the appointed place at which Druid Ceremonies were held locally. The location of the ceremony was in the opening of a cave surrounded by oak trees. It was clear that a ceremony was under way. A Chief Priest stood in the centre of the cave entrance behind a large white stone close to a second stone hollowed into containing rainwater.

In front of this stone was a fire where burnt offerings were placed around the head of a bull. In front of the burnt offerings sat a Priest with the skin of a bull draped around his shoulders reciting poetry, followed by a prayer to the One God.

The Chief Priest was standing behind the main stone adorned in a coloured robe. Priests and Priestesses stood on either side in white robes. After a brief ceremony, the Head Priest beckoned Joseph to come forward and the two sat together inside the cave entrance. The Head Priest explained to Joseph that he was aware that he, Joseph, was a wealthy and worthy man, and could afford to pay for the long training that would be necessary for his student Jesus to train to become a Druid Priest – seeker of truth, healer and teacher. Prolonged training was necessary because everything Druids' taught was learned in their heart and committed to memory. Every detail concerning the sacred duties to be undertaken by Druid Priests had to be committed to memory.

The Head Priest confided in Joseph the views of both himself and other priests who met Jesus; that Jesus was destined to reach the exulted position of Chief Druid Priest long before ten summers had passed, because everything about Jesus was in praise of the One God and the Reincarnation.

## AUTHOR'S NOTE:

Britain's Druids and the Romans

Fragmenting evidence from around the world dating back over 2000 years describes Britain as a land of religious warriors.

Tall, moustached warriors of great strength, education, civilised, trustworthy in trade, metal smelters of great skill. Britain was a manufacturing centre for metals and other goods of world renown. The truthful cameo of ancient Britains is far removed from the many lies and propaganda of the Roman Historians, and even our own early historians.

In very truth it was the Romans who were the barbarians from the most barbarous nation in the whole of Europe. The Romans lacked the knowledge or sense of moral right and wrong, never mastering the skills of the peoples they conquered. The Romans in reality were an inferior race of organised warmongers who plundered, slaughtered, and slaved; leaving a nasty stain on almost every country they conquered.

Romans left nothing of any real value in their wake, except heathen monuments to the extreme vanity of their leaders. Gods that could only have been dreamt up by the minds of those who enjoyed the ridiculous and sick spectacle of inhuman slaughter of slaves and animals in arenas for the enjoyment of their bloodthirsty masses. A very different picture to the Druidic communities in Britain who they destroyed in their familiar bloody revengeful acts of wanton murder and slaughter.

Jesus was well aware that he was a descendent of the Royal line of David, a Priest King. As he grew older, following in the footsteps of Joseph of Arimathea, Jesus himself became an authority on Jewish Law with a knowledge and understanding far in advance of his years. During Joseph's absence for many months during his return trips to the Far East, Jesus filled in as a speaker, travelling far and wide in the area learning as much as possible about local customs and belief systems.

In the sixteen years the trio spent in Cornwall they built a second Meeting House and became favourites of the Jewish community throughout the area. Such was their popularity they built their own wattle and daub meeting house on Glastonbury Tor, alongside the Druid Temple; for Joseph, Jesus and Joseph's son were all regarded by the Druids as holy men, worshipping the same God and provided goods and work for the local population. They also had customs in common, such as Baptism, and burnt offerings.

News of the Druids' Cornish success in mining and smelting Tin, Copper, Lead, Silver and Iron plus the valuable products from their fishing industry, already well known by the Romans, spread throughout Britain and across to Europe. Many more ships from ports in the South of Britain and from Gaul arrived in the Cornish ports to barter and trade. Some of the European crews were unscrupulous, and did not maintain the high standards set by the Jews.

After travelling and trading in Cornwall and Europe successfully for sixteen years the trio decided the time was right to return to Israel where they would be safer until the Roman Garrison in Cornwall had brought about some order to the mining areas.

Jesus looked forward to returning to Palestine in Spring, seeing the mass colour of Palestine in Bloom – crimson, pale blue, lilac, yellow, cream, purple and pink. Longing also to see his extended family once more to which he would most probably give the appearance of a fully matured Rabbi. Jesus knew that having been away for such a long period of time and gained so much knowledge, he was in danger of appearing as a perfect stranger to his own family. Nevertheless, Jesus was longing to reveal to the fishermen of Galilee the skills he had learned in Cornwall of which included new ways of netting fish; different methods of preparation and storing of fish, plus the oils that were the result of processing fish. Jesus was also enthusiastic about visiting and speaking at the Meeting Houses in Galilee and to see how they had grown in number. Jesus learnt much from the Druids about the casting out of evil, which was not known, in his own land and he looked forward to using this gift in Galilee.

Jesus returned to Galilee an exceptional man – confident, dynamic, worldly wise, an authority on world trade, alternative religions and an authority on Jewish Law, all of which made Jesus a spectacular and commanding speaker. Wealth acquired over 16 years enabled Jesus to recruit and support full time disciples and buy a house in Galilee. The ground floor of this house was used as a meeting place with benches around the outside walls and a centre table for food and wine and where the speaker would sit. The disciples lived in the upper rooms with their wives who were paid to keep house and cook the meals to support the group on their travels to other Meeting Houses (the first Jewish Synagogues). Female disciples helped with all the daily chores.

Some disciples recruited others to carry on with their fishing businesses whilst they were away. Using new methods taught by Jesus, which he had learnt in Cornwall, which helped their fishing businesses flourish.

Jesus was a huge success throughout Galilee. Teaching wisdom never before heard in Galilee – casting out devils, healing the sick and giving away healing potions to those that needed them. Jesus always demanded that those who were healed should tell no one. Jesus clearly did not want any credit attached to himself, nor did he want to be known as a miracle healer to those listening. His authority when speaking and his ability to heal, Jesus was regarded as otherworldly. Even his own family did not recognise him as the son who had left Galilee for Cornwall, England sixteen years previously.

At the end of the day Jesus taught his disciples in private session but many had difficulty in understanding his message but followed him in awe. Jesus taught that the only way God, who was outside this world, could communicate with the faithful in the world, was through Holy Spirit during meditation and prayer.

Meditation was a subject the disciples did not understand. Jesus taught that they had to start out on this road with their minds open and pure. Their minds should be completely free from anger, lust, or any sin. To know God their minds had to be "still", for his Holy Spirit would not go near or by anyone who committed any sin including anyone who placed a stumbling block before his brother or was angry with his neighbour.

Jesus taught that God loved each and every one of us; good or bad and longed for sinners to return to the fold because while they were in sin they were cut off from communicating with him, and could not recapture the Holy Spirit. However, if they first put things right with those they had sinned against, and where this was not possible, they understood the wrong they had done and why it was wrong and repented and they were forgiven and could receive the Holy Spirit. No one in his Kingdom held any priority over those who returned to Faith for God loved every one of the faithful equally. However, Jesus warned that there could be no forgiveness for evil committed by priests, nor would his Holy Spirit return to them until after they had left the priesthood.

Those who remained faithful and clean could call upon the Holy Spirit of Healing in Meditation and Prayer to heal and cast out evil spirits of the afflicted in God's name. The dynamism and magnetism of Jesus was such that in a short space of time Jesus blazed a path to a new way. A new understanding of ancient Jewish Law that gentiles could call their own that did not contradict or replace Jewish Law.

Put simply, Jesus brought the 'GOOD NEWS'. Access direct to God was available to everyone without strings attached. Everyone could call upon the Holy Spirit who kept the commandments or who genuinely repented their sins – to heal, to guide, to help to comfort. Life after death was certain. Everyone would go on to a new life they deserved prepared by the way they lived their lives in the present.

Jesus taught his Disciples that illumination is conscious union with the powers of the universe. An attachment, said to take over a persons being and very existence, because they become linked into a sea of spirit and knowledge causing a change from within, bringing about a slow and definite illumination that shows on the outside, losing the ignorance of discord, strife, craftiness and lack of peace. Replaced by a powerful harmony of joyousness, love, awareness that something greater than themselves has been activated in their life. A relaxation, wholeness, completeness, banishment of fear, improved health, patience, perseverance, increased mental powers, and the certain knowledge that their soul would continue after death.

## AUTHORS THOUGHT FOR THE DAY

And did those feet in Ancient times
Walk upon Englands mountain green
And was the Holy Lamb of God
On Englands pleasant pastures seen
And did the countenance devine
Shine forth upon our clouded hills
And was Jerusalem builded here
Among those dark satanic Mills.

William Blake 1757 - 1827

# The Sea of Spirit

The sea of knowledge of everything that was and ever will be is always out there. Spiritual light, higher consciousness, knowledge greater than everything that is known on earth at the present time – all contained within the powers of the universe. The great prophets, Jesus and some of the disciples, all knew that through a way of living and thinking and meditation, it was possible to tap into the powers of the universe and see the future and perform miracles of healing and gain illumination about developments in the future. How to achieve this divine form of meditation and the results, which know no limitation that flow from this practice: each individual alone can only achieve this transformation, explained in the Bible as transfiguration.

There is however a warning – not to be in a hurry to teach or share this illumination, even with ones own family or wife if they were not prepared, but to stay within the group that have also achieved illumination or one maybe killed or harmed by evil people with evil minds.

Most important to every individual was to lead a life that would guarantee a good passage into the next world. For as men lead their lives in this world, so they were creating the peace to which their spirit will travel in the next life. Jesus commanded such worldly knowledge and biblical knowledge with such absolute confidence that he left the Temple Priests in Jerusalem feeling bewildered and insecure. Seeing Jesus as a threat to their authority, possessing great powers they could neither comprehend nor understand, they wanted Jesus killed.

# The Return of Joseph of Arimathea to Cornwall from Galilee after the Death of Jesus

Joseph of Arimathea returned to Cornwall with close members of his family, and a few disciples around 32AD; escaping Roman soldiers who had orders to arrest Joseph following the disappearance of the body of Jesus, also from escaping the persecution and murder of Christians in and around Jerusalem.

Josephs' friends and relatives in the Jewish community, plus Josephs' business interests established in Cornwall over a very long period, enabled Joseph to lead and support an evangelising Christian community around the mining and smelting areas. The group built their own church of wattle and daub, set on piles in the form of a Meeting House on Glastonbury Tor in Somerset. This Meeting House and Christian community is said to be the earliest outpost of the Christian faith outside Jerusalem. The band worked in harmony with and alongside the Druids on the site that was known to be a sacred and holy place from earliest known times.

### AUTHOR'S NOTE:

### BLACKTHORN

Joseph of Arimathea brought with him from Galilee the Blackthorn, which he planted at Wirral Hill, Glastonbury. The hardwood from the dense Blackthorn thicket was fashioned for tool handles used in Smelters. Joseph is said to have planted his staff into the ground, which grew up into the Blackthorn. The 3-4m high thicket flowers at Christmas.

POSTCARD DATED 1905
GLASTONBUY ABBEY, THE HOLY THORN

STAMP DEPICTING THE
THE HOLY THORN

# JESUS SPOKE OF THE HOLY SPIRIT IN A WARNING TO PRIESTS

*Ye Priests ye do evil speak. Ye twist God's words to suit your abominations. Ye hath made My House a whore. Ye are bold in your evil for ye shelter and do give succour as to your evil ones. Repent and clean My House or My WRATH shall be great upon you. My Holy Spirit shall flee far from you.*

*Ye Priests who never leave your seats in MY MEETING HOUSE. Ye are gluttons and sluggards. Ye hath left MY WORK undone. Ye hath been silent to the evil ones and given them free passage into MY HOUSE. Repent and confess and sweep MY House clean or ye shall be no more.*

*Ye Priests who do practice abominations in My House. My HOLY SPIRIT shall flee from your Priesthood. Never shall it return. Ye are whores. Confess and repent and change your ways or My Time and Eternity shall be taken from you and ye shall be no more.*

*Ye Priests who do practice evil abominations upon My little ones. Ye are the greatest of Whores. My HOLY SPIRIT shall flee from you. It is better ye had not been born for MY wrath is great. Confess and repent and flee from MY Priesthood or your time and eternity of reincarnation shall be lost to you for evermore.*

# SISTER KATARINA'S MIRACLE

My wife and I were staying in Jerusalem for the purpose of making a documentary to illustrate the important principal to both children and adults alike that Christians, Muslims and Jews have a God given right to follow their own beliefs without fear or favour and must learn to live in harmony and to respect each other's differences.

At first we found it difficult to obtain permission from the various church authorities to film at the locations we had chosen and scripted. Permission to film Mary's Tomb, and the steps built by the Crusader Knights leading down to the Tomb where the Crusaders uncovered the 'Jesus Scroll', proved difficult. Equally problematic was gaining a licence to film within the Holy Sepulchre itself built over Calvary. However our dogged determination won through, we filmed in both locations in the early hours.

We felt very privileged as we entered the Holy Sepulchre at six a.m. with our film crew. Our first pleasant surprise was to be greeted by a serene and seemingly elderly nun Sister Katarina, standing opposite the Altar of Crucifixion; her dark robe and beautiful ageless eyes lit only by candlelight; she looked like an Angel.

The huge domed building was cold in the early morning. We sat warming Katarina's hands whilst at the same time inviting Katarina to talk to camera about the process of being chosen to serve at what most nuns would regard as the most holy place on earth.

Katarina opened to camera describing her vision:

*" I was very ill lying in Miami Florida, and thought to be dying, when I had a vision of Holy Mary who told me that I would not die, but would serve God in Jerusalem. Then I saw a vision of the Old City of Jerusalem after which I made a miraculous recovery from my illness, and was transferred to Jerusalem, where I serve God every day".*

THE AUTHOR AND CREW FILMING AT CALVARY

I asked Katarina if I could have a button from her cardigan or coat, as it would be a special blessing to have a memento from someone so loved by God as to be chosen to receive such a vision, and to be sent on such a special mission. Katarina replied to my utter astonishment, "I have been waiting for you. I have the white stone for you. You will read the Urim and Thummin".

Katarina explained that the white stone was a piece of Calvary that came away in her hand when she was cleaning the top of Calvary in preparation for a glass cover to be fitted over the point where the true cross entered the natural rock.

Sylvia and I returned home to England to cut and edit seven hours of film to a programme length of forty minutes. When that important film was finished, we set about looking for a Urim and Thummin.

We set our precious piece of Calvary on a purple cloth blessed by a Priest of the 'Basilica of the Agony' at the foot of the Garden of Gethsemane in Jerusalem. Said the Lord's Prayer; a prayer for Repentance and Remission of Sins; asked a question to the Urim & Thummin and studied the reply. The whole thing was immensely exciting, but I confess to being very surprised when the answers to our question was accurate as accurate could be. However as time went by I was aware of a growing feeling of uncertainty about whether we were using the system for the right purpose. We both felt uncertain about the issue and stopped using the Urim & Thummin until something really important came along for which we needed special help and guidance.

I have used the system only once since that time, and it was to ask for the healing of a painful kidney stone. The pain slowly faded but the stone miraculously disappeared overnight, later confirmed by x-ray.

We wrote to Sister Katarina sending her an enlarged photograph as she appeared in our film, also asking if there was anything she needed. The inevitable reply was "serving God in Jerusalem was more than sufficient reward in this life".

THE CRUSADER STEPS AND FLOOR LEADING
TO HOLY MARY'S TOMB IN JERUSALEM
MOTHER AND FATHER ANN AND JOACHIM
ARE BURIED ON THE LEFT AND RIGHT OF THE STEPS

AUTHOR'S PHOTOGRAPH OF THE ALTAR OF CRUCIFIXION
IN THE HOLY SEPULCHRE IN JERUSALEM
TENDED BY SISTER KATARINA

CHRIST'S TOMB IN THE
HOLY SEPULCAR IN JERUSALEM

# Chamberlain of Normandy Emerges as famous Knight William Clinton

This family took their surname from Clinton…….. in the Valley Three Miles North from Woodstock, Oxford.

# NORMAN KNIGHT
# WILLIAM CLINTON

To understand fully how a Norman Baron emerged with the name William Clinton, and how his descendants rose to become a Prime Minister of England, Dukes, Earls, Lords of Manors, Admirals, Generals and Governors, emigrating from England to Ireland to America, it is necessary first to understand the true unpoliticised story of the conquest of England in 1066 and the consequences for English ruling classes who were replaced almost overnight by the Norman French and became a virtual province of Normandy but with a much more diverse and wealthier economy than Normandy enjoyed. This was an economy greater than the economy of all the provinces of France taken together, all to be shared by William and a few cronies.

Since I do not have to bear the academic cross of fearing to raise my head above the wall, and disagreeing with what has been the politically correct findings about the Battle of Hastings over the centuries; laid down in our most politically correct history books. It records that King Harold was the unlucky loser. My factual and unbiased view is that King Harold did not stand a 'cat in hell's chance' of winning the battle of Hastings. Harold took on the most feared War Lord in the whole of Europe, Duke William of Normandy; the best equipped army in Europe; the most experienced fighters in Europe. King Harold, on the other hand, was wholly unprepared with only 2/3rds of his army, most tired from the forced march returning from York.

No archers, absolutely essential in such a battle, and without troops in reserve to replace holes in his lines of defence, that King Harold and his men gave a good account of themselves is not in doubt. It is because they had so much to lose that Harold was foolish in the extreme to take on William and his army – is proved in the outcome. Harold lost, and so did England. What England did gain was the first Bill Clinton; as I shall go on to explain.

The defeat of England's King Harold at the Battle of Hastings in 1066 by Duke William - 'William the Conqueror' of Normandy, France, was disastrous for the English who, almost overnight had imposed upon the Anglo Saxon nation a new Norman Royal Family, in a new Norman ruling class, in which the Clintons played prominent roll. A new culture, and a new language used in the administration of the land and in the affairs of the Courts.

After the Coronation as King of England at Westminster Abbey, London, on Christmas 1066, King William claimed the whole of England for his own. He dispossessed all but a few English Dukes, Earls and Lords of their titles and their lands, which William gave to 200 ducal families from Normandy plus Abbeys and Bishoprics all to be occupied mainly as tenants. Every tenant rendered Knight service and provided fyre (part time soldiers). England became a feudal monarchy overnight (feudal from the word fee). Saxon England was much bigger and wealthier than Normandy, hence the land distributed by King William, or land held in his name bestowed real wealth on the recipients. Much greater wealth than was around in Normandy, which comprised mainly peasants and poor farmers in a pastoral society.

One of King William's closest allies with close family ties was a famous Knight, Count Tankerville, Chamberlain of Normandy. His original surname came from a place in Normandy, anciently called Haut Ville, Coletin, but he later changed his name to Tankerville, after the famous Knight, Count Tankerville who acquitted himself outstandingly during Pilgrimages (unofficial Crusades) to Jerusalem.

Destined for high office in England, due to his closeness to William the Conqueror, Count Tankerville of Normandy, was anxious to adopt an English family name, and chose the name Clinton, a name from a valley three miles north of Woodstock in the County of Oxford. These details are laid down clearly in our original manuscript. Clearly establishing the fact that the first William Clinton, from whom all other Clintons are descended, emerged in England in 1066 from the ruling clans in Normandy.

Our manuscript shows that the famous Knight William Clinton and his descendants rose to the very top of the English Aristocracy. One changing his name to get rid of the Norman prefix when he was to become Prime Minister of England under the name Pelham.

Nearly 1000 years later, another outstanding individual changed his name to the name of his stepfather. William Clinton travelled from America to Oxford, England, to attend Oxford University, before going on to become President of the United States of America. One of the most successful; most popular and best loved Presidents of our times, who achieved so much for America and did so much for peace in the world and is still a blessing on this earth. Many of Bill Clinton's important successes have never reached the American press.

Amazingly, Hillary Clinton the likely first elected female President of the USA is also "entangled in time" with English genes running though her veins.

Jonathon Rodham, a colliery overseer left County Durham in 1881 for the coalfields of Seranton, Pennsylvania. His grandfather was born at Chester le Street in County Durham in 1779.

It is astonishing that their descendent Emily Rodham, also born at Chester le Street, put on a costume, dressing as the Statue of Liberty for a town parade to celebrate the "American Land Lease Programme to send war supplies to Britain". She was apparently a really lovely woman like Hillary Clinton herself.

It appears to me that buried deep in Emily's mind was the reincarnation through to the present day Hillary Clinton, and what greater omen to Hillary Clinton's likely success in the Presidential race could emerge.

# KNIGHT WILLIAM CLINTON RECRUITS KNIGHTS FOR THE FIRST OFFICIAL CRUSADE

The Clintons hold some of the secrets unearthed by the Knights Templar in and around the Holy Lands.

Famous Crusader Knight William De Tankerville

# WILLIAM CLINTON ON A PERSONAL CRUSADE TO THE HOLY LAND

Knight William Clinton, Robert Duke of Normandy, (William the Conqueror's eldest son), his brother-in-law Stephen, Count of Blois and his cousin, Robert of Flanders, all set out on a personal crusade to honour King William 1$^{st}$ on the tenth anniversary of his death, and to show respect to the Pope for Rome's support for King William's campaign in England in 1066.

This group travelled separately from the main Crusade under Godfrey. Anticipating an absence of around three years, Robert, Duke of Normandy raised money by mortgaging the Duchy of Normandy to his younger brother, Rufus King of England.

To understand the determination and enduring qualities required of these knights and how the Clintons' came into possession of ancient sacred scrolls and treasures, we look through a potted history of the Crusades.

KEEPER OF WILLIAM THE CONQUERER'S HAWKS

A MASTER SMITH WHO TRAVELLED WITH
WILLIAM THE CONQUERER'S KNIGHTS

# THE CRUSADES

The Crusades were very successful in founding a Christian Kingdom in the Holy Lands, which lasted for nearly 200 years.

The Knights who volunteered for the first official crusade under Godfrey in 1076 came from every part of central Europe, England and Scotland. The Crusaders set out to travel mainly overland to Jerusalem, with a short sea journey from Venetia (Venice, Italy), and the Port of Brindisi in South East Italy (A Roman Naval Base). These ports were the two main gateways for the Crusades. The ships available were little more than crude sailing galleys that could sink from overloading. One galley did overturn with loss of pilgrims and animals from the first Crusade. These galleys sailed without charts or navigation from Brindisi to Dalmatia, along the beautiful mountainous coastal belt in West Yugoslavia with its many offshore islands; landing at Dubrovnik. Some of these ships were built in Cornwall, England.

After disembarking the Crusaders and Pilgrims then had to endure travelling through dense forest, and crossing fast running rivers with their horses, sheep and goats (their meat on the hoof). Pilgrims and animals died from drowning, exhaustion and disease before reaching the half way point on their travel, which was the town of Constantinople (formerly Byzantium, now Istanbul). With the hindsight of previous Crusades, which went under the guise of Pilgrimages before the first official Crusade, the Knights knew that at Constantinople the Byzantium Emperor, who had good political reasons for wanting the Crusader Knights to attack his enemies beyond the Turkish Borders, would supply them with food and other essentials. Without the help of the Emperor, it is unlikely that the Crusade would have made it through central Turkey and into the Holy Land in one journey.

The unarmed Christian Pilgrim stragglers, who failed to keep up with the leaders were robbed and murdered on the way through Turkey by armed Moslem bands to whom they were easy pickings. Many more lives were lost on the arduous journey across the Taurus Mountains. However, a pleasant surprise was in store for them when they reached the Christian Armenian towns. Crusaders and Pilgrims alike were welcomed with open arms and given food and water (Armenia was the first nation to adopt Christianity as a state religion)

Eventually the Crusade reached Syria the gateway to the Promised Land. The Knights lay siege to the City of Antioch for nine months. The fall of Antioch was heralded as a great triumph, for there lay before them the road down the valley to Jerusalem, and the coastal sea route to the Port of Jaffa. When the Crusade eventually reached Jerusalem there were less than 20,000 survivors from the original estimate of 100,000 or more pilgrims and Crusaders that set out on the quest. With the memory of the great numbers that perished on the way to Jerusalem from hardship, starvation, drowning, fever and murder by Moslems still fresh in their minds, the Knights set about providing a naval sea route back to Europe.

The Knights fought for and captured the Ports of Antioch, Sidon, Tyre, Acra and Jaffa. All the ports and harbours along the coastline down to the nearest port to Jerusalem which was Jaffa. The Knights then fortified these ports and harbours, which were previously open to easy attack. Jerusalem was fortified by the building of towers at strategic points.

On completion of a Crusade to the Holy Land, successful or otherwise, Lords Knights and their vassals, who were not staying on for fortification work, returned to their homeland, having been assured by their travelling priests of the remission of their earthly sins; they would return to attend to the duties of their estates. There were exceptions of course; notably amongst which was John de Mandeville, member of the de Mandeville family who rose to become Norman appointed Earl of Essex. John de Mandeville ventured beyond Jerusalem into Egypt searching for ancient scrolls and treasure, and allegedly wrote a book about his travels.

## AUTHOR'S NOTES

Princess Matilda, (1102 -67) daughter of Henry 1st of England (who designated her his heir) married into the Knights Templar in France with her second husband Jeffrey, Duke of Anjou. After which the French Templars travelled to England regularly, and set up the Temple Church in London in 1185. Using Temple Church as a base, Templar Knights travelled into Essex, Kent and the Midlands and beyond, and Salisbury in the west. All areas where they set up their normal business of storing and guarding crops, and selling seed in the planting season.

# THE FIRST OFFICIAL CRUSADE 1096 - 1099 LED TO THE CAPTURE OF JERUSALEM

Immediately the news of the success by Crusader Knights reached the Vatican Rome, it spread throughout Europe. Pilgrims keen to see the wonders of the Holy Land, and gain remission of their sins plus a blessing from a 'Pilgrimage up to Jerusalem', as it was described in there times, flocked to the Port of Jaffa.

Travel from the Port of Jaffa however, through Moslem territory was extremely dangerous and continued so for the 200 years the area remained under Christian control. Bands of Moslem robbers would pillage and rape groups of unarmed Pilgrims travelling past Moslem villages. In 1119 the treatment of pilgrims by Moslem robbers became so vile, that a band of nine Crusader Knights headed by Hughes de Payen, and Geoffrey de St Omer, set up a holy order of Saint Augustine monks, taking vows of poverty, obedience and chastity, to protect pilgrims travelling to Jerusalem. The Knights were housed in the al-Aqsa Mosque on the Temple Mount with the support and blessing of the Christian King of Jerusalem. Thus the order of Knights Templar was born.

Their official duty was "to escort pilgrims arriving in the Holy Land, and protect them from bands of armed Moslems. These duties continued until 1328 after the fall of most Crusader forts. A Papal Bull to the religious authorities in Cyprus stated that Knights were needed for duties elsewhere, and their role would be taken over by Franciscan Monks whose job it would be to escort and care for pilgrims. The Moslem robbers took advantage of this situation by attacking the unarmed pilgrims, stealing the monk's clothes so that they rode naked into Jerusalem. From Rome the Pope charged Kings and Nobles loyal to Rome to continue to outfit their Knights and their vassels for official Crusades to the Holy Land.

A second official Crusade was organized, and with the benefit of hindsight this Crusade was better planned and equipped than the first. Many knights, pilgrims, horses and supplies sailed from Brindisi direct to Crusader ports, which were captured and fortified along the coastal route to Jaffa.

THE AL AQUSA MOSQUE (DOME OF THE ROCK) JERUSALEM

# JAMES THE BROTHER OF JESUS

The Pope ordered the Knights to uncover the truth about the secretive religious sects in and around Jerusalem, rumours about which had reached his attention. The orders from Rome were to find the Holy Grail, relics of significances, such as the true cross, and the spear with which the Roman soldier pierced the side of Jesus as he hung on the cross. The Pope was also very interested in the rumours that ancient scrolls from independent sources confirmed that Jesus had a brother called James, who Jesus appointed to the task of running the church in Jerusalem. James did this successfully for over 30 years. James was the very first Christian Bishop. James was celibate, did not drink wine, did not eat meat, nor shave his head. James had a great influence over his people, and was known as the 'Teacher of Righteousness'. Romans in the Temple precincts while addressing a crowd stoned him to death. The self appointed Apostle Paul, a roman who hated James and attacked him frequently in his letters, was said to be the ringleader.

# Gold and Documents Uncovered in Jerusalem

Following the successful siege of Antioch, the Knights searched the Church of St Peter, where they uncovered the 'Lance of Destiny' that pierced the side of Jesus whilst he hung on the cross. The Templar Knights moved on into Jerusalem itself where they searched under the Dome of the Rock, uncovering some gold treasure thought to be from Solomon's Temple, plus the true cross, which they re-buried. They also uncovered a coded document attesting to the fact that the Arc of the Covenant was moved to Ethiopia for safety centuries earlier. Other artifacts uncovered were gold tablets thought to date back to the time of Solomon. These tablets were sent back to France, and went to America. These gold tablets were possibly those uncovered by Joseph Smith, in America; Founder of the Mormon Church.

Although the second Crusade failed in its attempt to capture the capital of Syria, the Crusades made gains in other areas such as Outreimer and Gaza, where they rebuilt the forts. However, eventually in the face of overwhelming numbers of Turks, Outreimer was lost, then Jerusalem and Gaza, followed by Acra in 1291 the last Temple stronghold in the Holy Lands. Although no one should doubt that the Knights Templar remained the best fighting force in the world, facing overwhelming numbers, failing supplies, disinterest in Rome, the Crusaders retreated to Europe with their treasures and ancient scrolls. The prospect of facing a sixth Crusade brought the Moslems to the negotiating table, and to everyone's surprise Jerusalem came back into Christian hands with Christian Moslem alliance. Nevertheless disputes between Crusaders and various Moslem factions were never resolved.

# Baron Clinton – Deputy Grand Master of the Knights Templar to King Edward 1

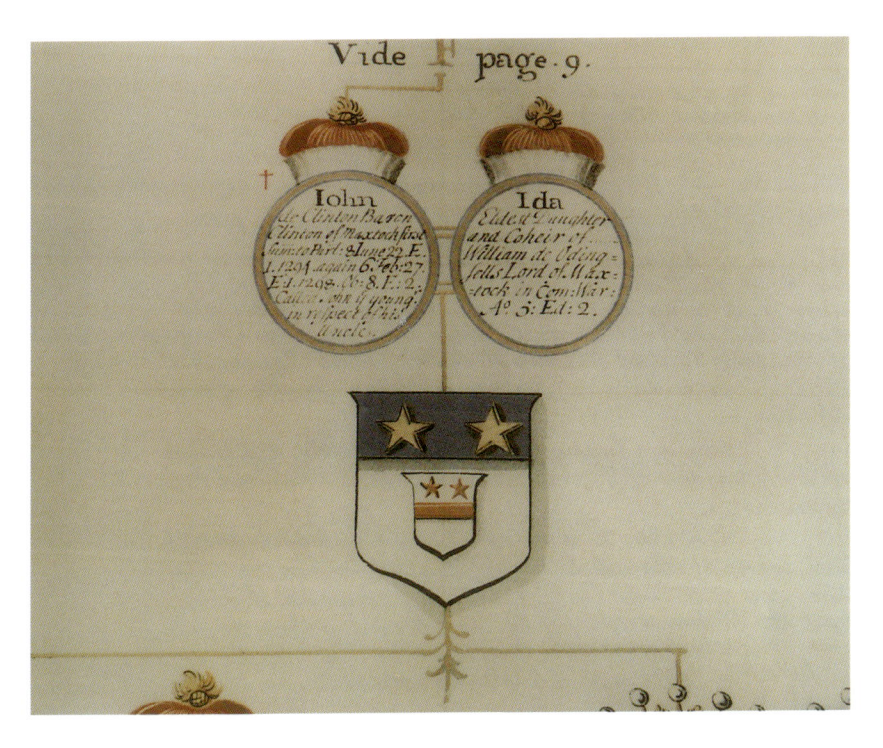

John de Clinton Baron Clinton of Maxstock, first summoned to Parliament 22 June 1294.

# THE KNIGHTS TEMPLAR
# VS
## BARON JOHN DE CLINTON

On the 12th May 1306 King Edward I attended Westminster where his son, Edward Prince of Wales was knighted at the high alter, appointed Duke of the Aquitaine, France, and Master of the Order of the Knights Templar in England. On the following day Baron John De Clinton, Deputy Grand Master of the Order of the Knights Templar, attended the Prince of Wales. Together, the Grand Master and his Deputy invited all single inherited Knights, sons of Earls, Barons and Lords of Manors to attend New Temple in London; to don their golden robes for their investiture into the Order of Knights Templar after which they were to keep vigil at Westminster to confirm their vows. This was the largest investiture of Templar Knights in Europe.

## THE RITUALS OF THE ORDER

The rituals of the Order obligated the newly invested Templars to take on the moral and religious obligations of the Order, which included Chastity, vows to defend the Holy Land, to protect pilgrims, to regard the Order of the Knights Hospitallers whose duty it was to care for the poor and sick pilgrims travelling in the Holy Lands. Another of the Knights duties was to raise funds for crusades to Jerusalem.

## REMISSION OF EARTHLY SINS

In return for carrying out their obligations and duties to the Order of the Knights Templar, Knights were promised remission of their earthly sins, and the privileged position of being beyond the jurisdiction of any Court of Law or religious Court. The Knights were answerable only to the Pope. The Knights were responsible for supplying and maintaining their own Sergeants and Esquires.

A TEMPLAR KNIGHT AT CRESSING TEMPLE BARNS IN ESSEX, ENGLAND – BARRING THE WAY TO THE CHAPEL DURING A CEREMONY OF INVITATION

A YOUNG TEMPLAR KNIGHT PATROLS THE GROUPS OF
CRESSING TEMPLE BARNS

## Templars Onshore Tax Haven

Landowners granted properties to the Order ostensibly for the safe storage of crops such as wheat and barley. One might wonder at the generosity of the wealthy farmers until one realizes that the Knights Templar were running what would be described today as an onshore tax haven. Templars were exempted from paying taxes or disclosing their business privileges. This greatly annoyed the King of England and the King of France as obviously the loss of revenue involved was great. Farmers and merchants alike gained all round from doing business with the Templars. They did not pay tax on their profits, and their goods and crops were in safe storage in Templar Barns. The death sentence would be metered out to anyone foolish enough to try and steal from their barns. The Templars also acted as brokers; selling seed to farmers at planting times.

## The Templar Wealth

The Knights Templar became enormously wealthy from the proceeds of their seven main activities; Transportation, Safe Storage and Brokering Seed, Banking, Money Lending, Safety Deposit, Money Laundering.

AN ANGLO SAXON WIFE AT CRESSING TEMPLE MAKING
CORDS FOR FIXING SHOES AND JERKINS IN 1265

AN ANGLO SAXON MERCENARY IN THEPAY OF THE TEMPLER
KNIGHTS GUARDING PRODUCE AFTER HARVEST

# CRESSING TEMPLE BARN, ESSEX, ENGLAND

The finest surviving example in England is a Wheat Barn dated 1220 and a Barley Barn dated 1260 are at Cressing Temple Barns in the County of Essex, England. Temple Cressing was also a commandery in 1338, which was an administrative unit of the Order of St Johns Hospitallers, (A two-hour car journey or one-hour train journey from central London). The barns were sacked in 1381 during the Peasants Revolt and it is a miracle they survived. The end came in 1541 with the Dissolution of the Monasteries, when the Knights Templar left the site. An Elizabethan house was built on the site, and part of this house remains at the Cressing site today. Fortunately for posterity the barns have been restored to their former glory, and maintained as a place of special interest. There are re-enactments of the Templar Fairs on the site from time to time, which enable the public to get a feel of the atmosphere pervading these fairs all those centuries ago.

Anyone interested in history owe a debt of gratitude to Essex County Council for preserving and restoring these most important barns. Essex Parks Department also deserve a note of praise for bringing the history of the site alive through the many functions taking place throughout the year for the benefit of children and adults alike.

## CRESSING

Queen Matilda gave the Cressing site to the Templars in 1137, which became the largest and most important estate in Essex. The Templars commissioned two of the largest timber barns in Europe, which are standing there today.

CRESSING TEMPLE BARN - WHEAT BARN

CRESSING TEMPLE BARN - BARLEY BARN

THRESHING IN THE WHEAT BARN IN THE 13TH CENTUARY
INTENTIONALLY LEFT BLANK FOR PHOTOGRAPH

ANGLO SAXON CARPENTER AND APPENTICE RIGGING THE
WHEAT BARN IN 1290

## Baron Clinton Warns the French Templars of Their Impending Destruction

## Gold Tablets Unearthed in Jerusalem Sail for America Leading to the Birth of the Mormon Church

## The Templar Bank

The major Bank in Europe created by the Knights Templar was the Temple Bank in Paris. The Temple Bank had come to the rescue of the French King, and supported Rome for decades. The French King needed the Templar Bank. France was mainly a poor peasant farming community, much as it is today outside the main centres, consequently producing low revenue from taxes and high unemployment. The Papacy needed the Templar Bank because much of the monies pledged to Rome to support Crusades were never paid. Many of the wealthy French farmers and landowners who should have paid taxes to the Crown avoided so doing, by storing their commodities with the Knights Templar who were exempted by Rome from paying duty or taxes.

It is not therefore entirely surprising that the French King, who was always in debt as a result of his extravagant life style, resented the Templars privileges; was happy to conspire with Rome to outlaw the Order of Knights Templar. One result of which would be an increase in taxes paid to the King. Seizing the treasures and property belonging to the Order was to his mind fair recompense for the taxes avoided by wealthy farmers. But the most satisfying result from outlawing the Order and imprisoning the leaders would be that the huge debts owed by the French King and Rome would never have to be repaid. The torture and murder of the Knights Templar is one of the most outrageous and vile events in European history.

## Friday the 13th

On Friday 13th, 1307 King Philip of France ordered the arrest of the Templars, with the order that those arrested should be tortured until they confess their alleged heretical practices. The heretical crimes of which they were accused were 'spitting upon the cross', idolatry, homosexual practices and more. There was no actual evidence put forward of such practices. In truth, the Pope was angered by the information coming from his Catholic Priests travelling with the Templars, that the Templars were following their own ceremonies and versions of religious doctrine from scrolls they had uncovered in and around Jerusalem quoting the teachings of James, the brother of Jesus. The Templars were ignoring their own Catholic Priests and not attending Catholic Mass or Communion.

# MORMON CHURCH IS INDEBTED TO TEMPLAR KNIGHTS

The French King invited England's' King Edward 1 to join with the French and collaborate on the destruction of the Templars. The English King was no lover of King Philip of France, who was constantly a thorn in his side. King Edward instructed Baron Clinton to warn the Templars in France of their impending destruction. This warning gave dozens of Templars sufficient time to flee to their ships with ancient scrolls and treasures. In a wide dispersal they fled to Scotland, Ireland, Norway, Sweden, Spain, Germany and America. This was one of the greatest dispersals of ancient scrolls and treasures in history. The gold tablets brought from Jerusalem are almost certainly those uncovered by Joseph Smith in America, which lead to the birth of the Mormon Church in America.

The blurring of the difference between the ceremonies and the rites of the different Orders suited the French King and the Pope at that time. The Order of Knights Templar was dissolved, Six Templars were executed, and its Grand Master languished in prison for seven years before being executed. These Templar Knights were executed in France for crimes they did not commit. The murder of the innocent Knights, who had fought for the Christian cause in the Holy Lands, had lived a life of chastity and obedience to their leaders and the church, weighted heavily on the conscience of the Papacy. In the fourteenth century, Pope Clement took the decision to purge the Vatican of these grave sins by issuing a pardon for the Templars who had been murdered by a conspiracy backed by Rome at that time.

The Templars existed in a time of lawlessness and distrust and lack of understanding for different languages. It was, therefore, by necessity a secret order. The original Knights Templar were of noble birth, bound by oath and honour. Due to the many knights killed on campaigns it became necessary to recruit members from the lower classes. As long as they could acquit themselves well in battle, they would qualify for membership. It therefore became necessary to bind this class of member to the Order, certified by initiation rituals and secret code.

One of the results of the expansion of members was an increase in the number of properties controlled by the Order to around 10,000, many of them fortified buildings or churches, many of them containing treasure. It was therefore easy for the Order to continue in France, underground, after being dissolved. One result was the increased use of secret codes and ciphers, many brought back from Egypt.

An ancient letter indicates that the Knights Templar did uncover a treasure of many ancient scrolls in the Holy Land, some of which were not handed over to the Papacy, or Kings who financed the Crusades. The more interesting scrolls were kept by Grand Masters to embellish and enhance the devotions and teachings of the Crusader Monks, and taken back to the Order headquarters in Europe. An ancient letter states that the last resting place of the Arc of the Covenant was in Ethiopia where it was taken for safekeeping.

The head of the Roman Lance that pierced the side of Jesus went with a small part of the treasures to Scotland when the Knights fled from France to escape their imminent arrest. A cup said to be used by Jesus and his Disciples at the Last Supper, was sent with a trusted Italian Knight to Rome, but whether or not it reached Rome we do not know. There were several cups of different shapes and sizes brought back by the Knights from Jerusalem, all claimed to be the cup used by Jesus at the Last Supper.

Some of the charges levelled against the Templars by the French King and Papacy at the time of their arrest were criticisms of the forms of the rituals and religious rites practiced by the Templar groups. However, the accusers twisted the facts. The practices they criticized were those used in the ceremonies by the German Teutonic Knights Sword Brothers, Rituals borrowed from those described in ancient manuscripts unearthed in the Holy Land. Original ceremonies used by the Priests of the Moon Goddess. A religion practiced in Arabia when Moses arrived with the Exodus. Moses followed the well-trodden trade routes to waterholes. Indeed it was recorded that Moses was a guest of the High Priest of the Moon Goddess soon after his arrival. Other scrolls from quite independent sources, some in Syria and Aramaic recorded the life of James, the brother of Jesus, known as the Teacher of Righteousness, and the disciplined life of James and his many followers.

Ancient scrolls reveal that the original pure Aryan peoples who came into Europe in the Second Millennium BC were blond with fair skin and blue eyed. These peoples brought with them their ancient rituals, rites and practices, which included the chanting of holy songs, meditation, healing and revealing hidden things. They are said to have possessed divine sacred knowledge, and their emblem was what we know today as the Swastika. Some of their number migrated to Northern India, but the majority settled in Israel before Christ was born.

They separated themselves off into their own secretarian movement. Their teachers remained celibate, but this was not required of their followers. All practiced meditation, chastity and healing. None ate meat or took strong drink.

CRAFTSMAN TRAVELLING WITH THE KNIGHTS

# THE CLINTONS LED THE KNIGHTS TEMPLAR TO MELT UNDERGROUND INTO FREEMASONRY

AUTHOR'S PHOTOGRAPH

The Lithostrotos – original Roman pavements where the Roman soldiers held Jesus and dressed him in a Crown of Thorns after playing the game of King. The pattern of the game is recorded on early Freemasonry badges.

# THE KNIGHTS TEMPLAR WENT UNDERGROUND BUT CONTINUED TO BE HEADED BY CLINTONS

The Knights Templar and Knights Hospitallers disappeared underground in all the countries to where the Templars had dispersed. Keeping themselves as very secret Orders basically in two camps: The Knights Templar of the Temple Mount and Sepulcher, and the Knights of St John of the Red Cross of Jerusalem. These Orders gave rise to Seculchre Orders being established in England; The Garter, Thistle, Bath, St Michael and St George. These Orders were offered only to the very top echelon of Society with Royal or Political connections. As to the ordinary lodges, no records were kept in England, Scotland or Ireland until 16th Century.

In Germany information was recorded from the 14th Century. Most early Kings of England, or their Princes were Grand Masters of the Lodges, but after George I the honour befell the oldest Duke, and in the 1800's the Duke of Kent became Grand Master, a tradition that has continued until the present day. King George 1st decided to revive the Order when members were dying out from epidemics and plagues. King George made eligible for membership all craftsmen with the highest quality work. This move evoked the spread of lodges to every corner of England, Scotland and Ireland. During the 1700's lodges began to keep records and became more organized. There were four lodges in the City of London and Westminster with the famous Christopher Wren becoming a Freemason.

Noblemen, gentleman of high rank, clergymen, judges, lawyers, accountants and other professionals, including master craftsmen (who made up a large section of lodge members) were invited to join. Members were obligated to attend dinners and wear lodge regalia and badges after initiation. London lodges held their meetings at the Goose and Gridiron Alehouses, St Paul's churchyard, Crown Alehouse, Parkers Lane, Drury Lane, Rummar and Grapes Tavern, in Channel Row, Westminster, Apple Tree Tavern. The great distances, and time it took to travel between London, York and Edinburgh, due to bad roads and highwaymen meant that lodges were not yet in communication or organized into area memberships.

# DEVELOPMENT OF FREEMASONRY

All Freemasonry has legitimate origins dating back thousands of years to the building of the Temple of Solomon, and forward to the execution of Jesus and the murder of his brother James by the Romans. The Masonic Lodges that have grown up over the centuries can be separated into two different groups, each with different origins and purpose. The original Order of the Knights Templar that served in the Far East, and fled from the French ports to avoid arrest and imprisonment, were a religious order with sophisticated interests in commerce, banking and philosophical enlightenment. They set up Masonic Lodges in the following countries, and enjoyed a period of growth into the fourteenth century:

| France | Sweden | Scotland | Spain |
| Ireland | Germany | Norway | North America |

The Orders are very secretive and have continued existence up to the present. They use basically the same rites, symbols and codes brought back from the Holy lands. Whether they continue to own the sacred manuscripts uncovered there we do not know. Nevertheless they can be identified by the designs of the jewellery on their regalia. One design is the engraving of the layout for the game of King. Carved on the original Roman paving stone in the Lithostrotos off the Via Dolorosa (the route where Jesus carried his cross). The Romans played the game of 'King' with finger knucklebones (similar to five stones) The winner had the power of life and death over the prisoner, and could chair a debate on his fate. In the case of Jesus, the Roman soldiers decided to dress Jesus with a crown of thorns. Other symbols used by the Knights Templar Masons were jewelled scenes of Jesus with his cross; walking the Via Dolorosa (the route to the Holy Sepulchre).

# MODERN DEVELOPMENT OF FREEMASONRY

The other Masonic lodges that appeared and expanded in number in the eighteenth century when communications and travelling improved and became relatively safe, had their origins in the Mark Masons in Solomon's time. Their jewellery and symbols are mainly, 'The Eye of Horus', calipers, set squares and all things engineering.

Solomon formed alliances with Egypt, and the Phoenicians on the coastal plain of Syria. All these areas fell under his influence, and Solomon built the Temple at Jerusalem on Temple Mount. Mark Masons were important craftsmen in these areas, and stuck together in self interest family groups, monopolizing all the work available, and seeing that the work was carried out to a high standard. Masonic Lodges whose origins came down from Solomon continue into the present day, but they are quite different to the Lodges set up by the Knights Templar in both their purpose and their aims.

# COMMON DESCENT OF

# GEORGE WASHINGTON
# AND
# WILLIAM SPENCER CHURCHILL

America's greatest and most successful presidents are products of their ancient English genes.

This window is erected to the memory of the Revd Lawrence Washington, Rector of Purleigh, the Great-great-grandfather of George Washington, the first President of the United States of America. Buried in this Churchyard January XXI MDCLII.

This memorial is the gift of the Citizens of Malden, Massachusetts, and a Committee of the Sulgrave Institution, U.S.A., whose names are recorded in a book deposited in the Archives of this Church. MCMXXVIII.

# KEY PEDIGREE
### shewing the common descent from
## ROBERT KYTSON
### of George Washington and Winston Spencer-Churchill

**Robert Washington** of Tewitfield in Warton, Lancs. — **Robert Kytson** of Warton, Lancashire

JOHN WASHINGTON ~ MARGARET KYTSON     Sir THOMAS KYTSON
of Hengrave, Suffolk, died 1540

LAWRENCE WASHINGTON     KATHERINE ~ Sir JOHN SPENCER
Circa 1500-1585     KYTSON 1545 of Gt. Brington, buried there 1586
Builder of Sulgrave Manor

Sir JOHN SPENCER
buried 1599

WALTER LIGHT     ROBERT     ROBERT SPENCER
of Radway ELIZABETH ~ WASHINGTON     1st Baron Spencer, buried 1627
Grange,     died 1599     1540-1620
Warwickshire     of Sulgrave, buried there     WILLIAM SPENCER
2nd Baron, died 1637

HENRY SPENCER
1st Earl of Sunderland

LAWRENCE WASHINGTON     ROBERT SPENCER
Circa 1568-1616     2nd Earl, killed 1643
Buried at Brington, Northamptonshire

JOHN CHURCHILL ~ SARAH JENNINGS
1st Duke of Marlborough

Rev. LAWRENCE WASHINGTON     HENRIETTA     ANNE ~ CHARLES
M.A., B.D., Circa 1602-1653     Countess of Godolphin     CHURCHILL SPENCER
Fellow of Brasenose College, Oxford 1623-1633     3rd Earl of Sunderland
Rector of Purleigh     1674-1722
Buried at Maldon, Essex

CHARLES SPENCER
5th Earl of Sunderland, 3rd Duke of Marlborough, 1706-1758

Colonel JOHN WASHINGTON     GEORGE SPENCER
1633-1677     4th Duke of Marlborough, 1739-1817
Settled in Virginia

GEORGE SPENCER
5th Duke of Marlborough, 1766-1846
(Assumed the name of Spencer-Churchill in 1817)

Captain LAWRENCE WASHINGTON     GEORGE SPENCER-CHURCHILL
1659-1698, of Virginia     6th Duke of Marlborough, 1793-1857

JOHN SPENCER-CHURCHILL
Captain AUGUSTINE WASHINGTON     7th Duke of Marlborough, 1822-1883
1694-1743, of Virginia

RANDOLPH SPENCER-CHURCHILL
1849-1895

General GEORGE WASHINGTON     Sir WINSTON SPENCER-CHURCHILL
*President of the United*     *Prime Minister of the United*
*States of America.*     *Kingdom.*

**KEY PEDIGREE SHEWING THE COMMON DESCENT FROM ROBERT KYTSON**

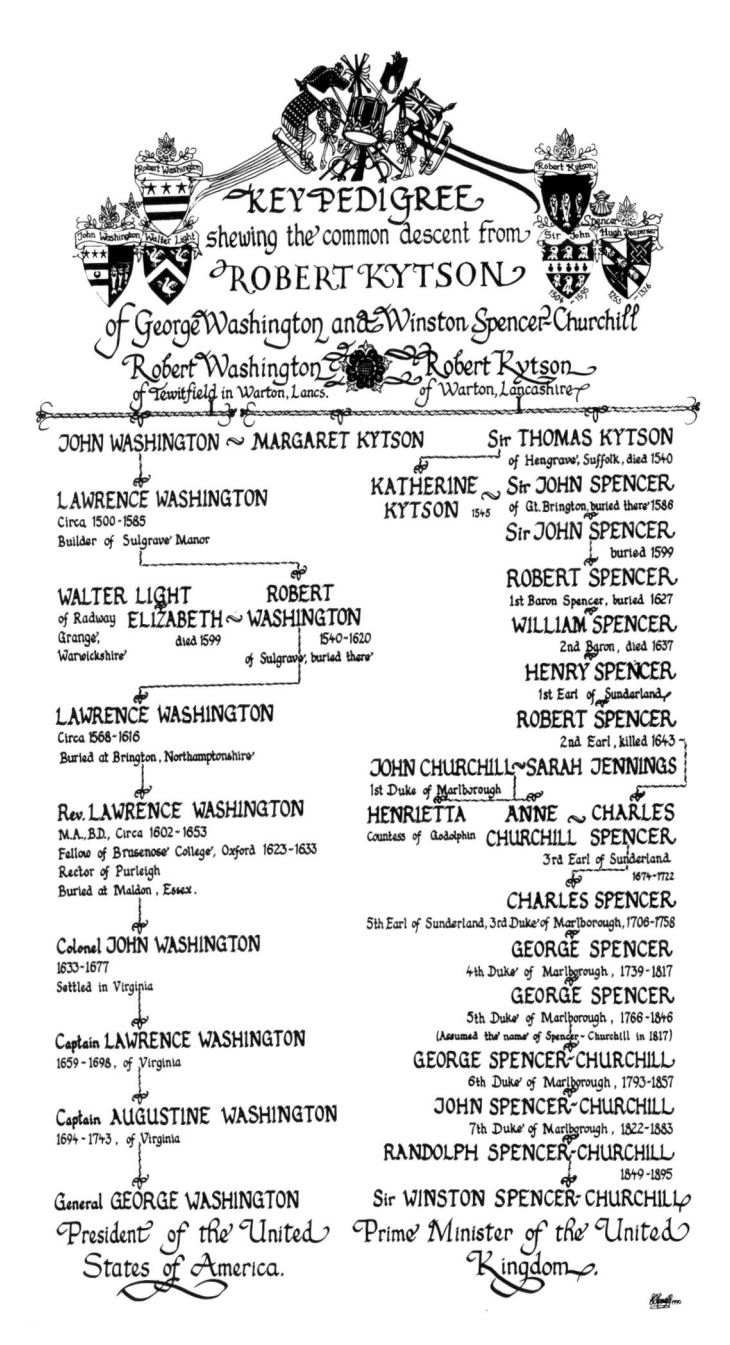

# The Clintons in Ireland
## Irish love of America and Canada

# IRELAND

In the ninth century, Ireland was a community of tribes and petty kings thriving in a simple and entirely pastoral economy. The churches and monasteries were the repositories of wealth, food, livestock, money and land. Rivalry between churches and monasteries was intense occasionally sufficiently intense to boil over into violence. Monks from rival monasteries would fight each other to the death. In times of famine, local people would also raid monasteries, some fatalities occurred as a result.

The middle of the ninth century was a dark period for Churches and Monasteries alike. Ruthless pagan Viking raiders regarded the ecclesiastical wealth as easy pickings, and the frequency of Viking raids intensified. Eventually Vikings settled and introduced their own farming communities into Ireland. They brought in skilled craftsmen and merchants. These events had an important influence on progressing the Irish economy from pastoral to partly mercantile. The most important of these developments was the introduction of technology and the skills to build large wooden vessels, plus the knowledge of the use of navigation to take those ships to and from Europe for trade. Previously the Irish used hide covered currachs, which were obviously confined to local use.

The Vikings established Dublin as a prosperous fortified town, with ships from Dublin trading far and wide bringing back more craftsmen and merchants from European countries to share in the prosperity that Dublin offered.

Dublin continued to grow into the pre-eminent centre of trade in Ireland. Other centres of wealth also developed in Limerick and Waterford, followed by Wexford and Wicklow. Dublin traded and exported everything from textiles, lace, wine, gold fabric and the most beautiful ornamental metalwork and jewellery. Pieces of which have been uncovered in digs throughout Europe.

Petty Irish Kings continued their never ending squabbling, sometimes fighting with the Vikings for control of Ireland. Coincident with the Norman invasion of England in 1066, Viking influence began to fade as they migrated to pastures new such as Kyiv, and Novgorod in Ukraine, and to the tip of America in the West.

A hundred years later Norman soldiers were invited into Ireland by Chieftain Dermot McMurrough Kavanagh, and the Norman took over the seat of control from the Vikings shaping the future of Ireland for the better.

The Irish suffered centuries of invasion and domination from England. Agricultural land on which the population depended was in the hands of a few landlords in the ruling classes. A farm tenants home in those days was very basic and austere. It measured five meters by four meters, with a fireplace, bed, chest for tools and a potato bin. Alongside these hardships there grew up a religious divide responsible for much cruelty and persecution, which was to last for centuries. Nevertheless, such was the natural resilience and determination of the Irish peoples that the population grew to be the most populous in Europe.

By 1841 there were eight million Irish. Ireland was overcrowded and undercapitalized. There were no railways, and all communications were poor. In truth the Country could not sustain such a large population. Fortunately, one of the benefits of a pastoral economy was that most people grew their own food, which they used for bartering and in exchange for services, but this way of living did not raise tax revenue for the Government. The Irish were desperately unlucky in that the main staple of their diet was the potato. As we know, the potatoes suffered a prolonged blight, and in 1846 three quarters of the nationwide crop rotted in the ground, which resulted in a nationwide famine, and sadly nearly a million people died.

Missing in English school history books is the fact that it was the greed and cruelty of the English and Irish ruling classes who were responsible for the deaths of a million in Ireland. Ireland was turned into a wheat growing country for the benefit of the English. The Napoleonic Wars caused prices of wheat in Europe to rise, but the English masters kept this profit. The Irish peasant received only sufficient from his wheat crop to pay his rent, and had to grow potatoes to feed his family. When prices fell after the Wars, the Irish peasant had to increase production of wheat to pay his rent. Those who could not were evicted without ceremony, because there was always someone who was starving ready to take the evictee's place.

When the Irish were dying in their hundreds of thousands, English troops protected the export to England of half the agricultural crops produced in Ireland. When the potato crops failed, food that could have prevented the deaths of hundreds of thousands of Irish people was exported for profit. America came to their aid even in those days. The Shakers of Ohio's Union Village sent a thousand bushels of corn.

It was a bewildering situation for Prime Minister Peel, and he ignored opposition from England and at Home, and spent money distributing maize imported from the Americas. Nevertheless, between 1852 - 61 around a million of the Irish population perished - a great tragedy. Another million were spared by escape to America and Canada from the terrible problems at home. English history books record an illusion that it was all the fault of the potato blight.

# The Canadian Connection

Canada was a destination of choice long before the potato famine. The Irish were a founding people of Canada. Millions of Canadians are descended from Irish (Viking) stock. After just twenty years of Irish immigration around a quarter of the Canadian population spoke with Irish accents. No one should doubt that the Irish did nothing but good for Canada. Taming the wilderness and shaping the country to what it is today. Over time conditions improved on ships transporting Irish immigrants to Canada. There was more space per person. The food improved, and luxuries such as tea, sugar and milk became affordable. Conditions luring doctors, surveyors and other professionals to follow the immigration trail.

# The American Connection

America was also a saviour to the Irish. Three fifths of all immigrants sailed for America, and many arrived penniless and almost naked during the famine period, but were still made welcome. Many able bodied young Irish lads were allowed to join the army after swearing an oath of allegiance.

Later in the period, Irish immigrants arrived adequately clothed, and with some money. This was a far cry from comparable scenes during the famine. Those who found work and prospered sent money home to their families in Ireland - monies totalling hundreds of thousands of pounds annually.

This money sustained their relatives at home in Ireland, paying off rents and debts. Many who returned home for holidays spoke about the good life in America, investing some money back home which encouraged the immigration to continue. The Irish have always been bright optimistic people with fire in their belly, and many went on to make good in America. Millions of good Americans have their origins in Ireland. Some have traced their ancestors, but those who have not can be confident that they inherited a strong pool of genes to die for. What Irish man today could ever hold back from saying "God Bless America", and not mean it with every ounce of his being.

# CLINTONS IN IRELAND

Edward Lord Clinton and Say
Lord Admiral of England and Ireland and Wales. Earl of Lincoln 1584

Elizabeth daughter of Gerald Fitz Gerald, Earl of Kildare 3rd wife

Katherine 2nd daughter. Wife of William
Lord Burgh Father of Thomas Lord Burgh and Deputy of Ireland

1795 Sir Henry Clinton, General and Commander in Chief of His Majesty's Forces in North America. Governor of Limerick.

Anna Maria Clinton and Harriot Susan Clinton, born in 1807 and 1809 respectively to Captain of the parish of Saint Peter, Dublin. Their sister Maria Augusta was born in Chester, England in 1799, before their father's transfer to Dublin, Eire. Two of the sisters were believed to have travelled to America in the 1930's.

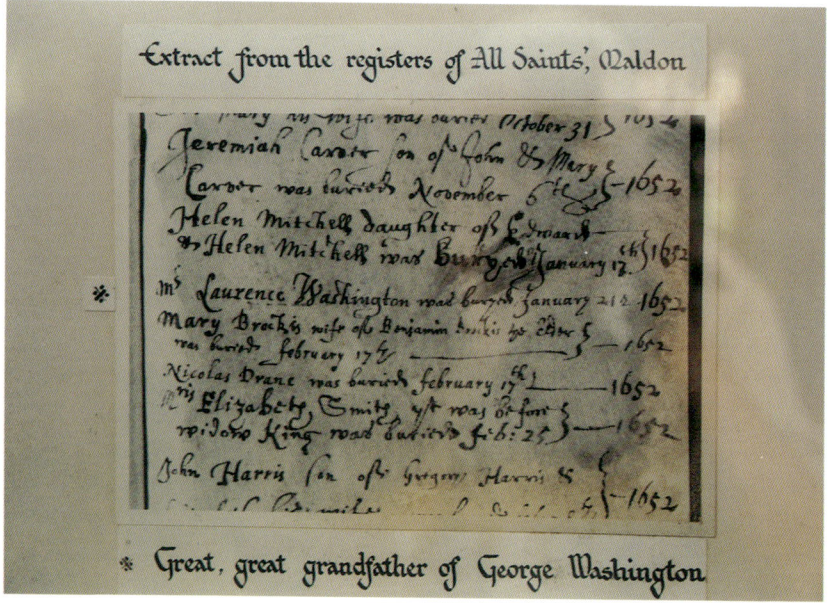

ALL SAINT'S CHURCH, MALDON, ESSEX, ENGLAND

# GOLDEN AMERICAN PRESIDENTS AND GENERALS WITH ENGLISH ANCESTORS AND THEIR ENGLISH GENES

## GENERAL GEORGE WASHINGTON

Two generals, both with English genes washing through their veins fought on opposing sides during the American War of Independence, one becoming the first President of the United States of America.

The two generals were: General Sir Henry Clinton born into the top echelons of the English nobility. Opposing was the first American President General George Washington, the great great grandson of English preacher Lawrence Washington, from the village of Purleigh, in the County of Essex, England. Formerly of Thrapston Church, and Sulgrave Manor, the family seat.

A few kilometers journey from the Rectory where Lawrence Washington lived, the ancestors of another great family name – Bush, a successful and wealthy English farmer, living in the village of Stisted, Essex, not far from Cressing Temple, the home of the Knights Templar at Cressing, Essex. The Bush's' were a devoutly religious family, much loved and respected in their village.

Not too distant in Oxford, England, a famous Knight, who adopted the English name William Clinton, intermarried into the very top of English nobility and whose offspring went on to sire children in Ireland, and emigrated to the Americas.

Sir Henry Clinton – General and Commander in Chief of His Majesty's Forces in North America

Author's photograph of the "ancient Port of Maldon, Essex" as seen in the present time.

English Preacher Lawrence Washington was dispossessed of his living at his Rectory in the small Essex Village of Purleigh over religious persecution. Lawrence moved a few kilometers away to the ancient Port of Maldon, Essex, where he ended his days. Lawrence Washington is buried in the churchyard of St Peters Church, Maldon. There is a commemorative stained glass window in the church donated by the people of Maldon, Massachusetts, USA, noting his death and depicting his great, great grandson George Washington signing the Declaration of Independence.

In 1657, Lawrence Washington's son John left Maldon, Essex and sailed for Plymouth Rock, Massachusetts, in that famous ship the Mayflower. About twenty-seven years earlier the ancestors of the Bush's sailed from the ancient Port of Maldon, Essex to Plymouth, Devon, to join the Mayflower, which departed for New England in 1620. Christopher Jones, Master of the Mayflower was also from the ancient Port of Maldon in Essex, where he was christened before his family moved to Harwich where his father was a successful ship owner and sea captain.

## ESSEX WIVES FOR SALE

Over one hundred years later at the same church in Purleigh, Essex where Lawrence Washington preached, a record of a baptism in 1782 mentioned a mother in the village was a 'bought' wife. Husbands in Essex and London paying off their debts or ending an unhappy marriage were selling their wives at market places to the highest bidder - a practice that continued until the end of the nineteenth century. A wreath was woven from ribbon and straw and placed around the women's necks to identify them to potential bidders. The husband would then call out the woman's virtues. A woman sold at rural markets could bring as much as ten shillings. Busy farmers and farm workers (in what was a successful and prosperous area) who had no time for courting, were happy to pay the equivalent of about one dollar. An attractive and lively Essex woman taken to a London Auction could fetch double and more, whereas a plump Midlands lass may fetch as little as five pence. A Scottish woman with a froward mouth brought a record low of four pence.

The practice of selling unwanted wives stemmed from the activities in the slave trade, which continued in England until 1834, a fact strangely omitted from English school history books. Privately owned domestic slaves were not uncommon in the households of the ruling classes, and they were bought and sold as chattels and goods. Men from London and Essex regarded their wives in the same light.

In 1834 an Act of Parliament made slaves completely free and the government paid compensation totalling millions of pounds to their owners, but the slaves received nothing. The selling of wives stopped about the same time a law was passed forbidding husbands regarding their wives as their chattels and goods. Divorce Courts were not set up until 1857. It would be fascinating to speculate just how much an attractive, lively, Essex wife would make at auction today, but I shall resist that despicable temptation.

## BACKGROUND ON ESSEX, ENGLAND
## THE GARDEN OF EDEN

Parts of the County of Essex, England, are perhaps the most underrated within the English counties. Essex has enjoyed a warm dry climate from the Roman times. Good for ripening and drying seed. Excellent for growing fruit and produce. All stored and distributed widely by the Knights Templar from Cressing Temple barns at Cressing in Essex. For the record, Essex also has the longest coastline of any English County.

## ESSEX VILLAGES PROSPER

The areas famous for seed cultivation were the villages around Coggeshall, Cressing, Feering and Messing. Fruit growing was the prominent feature of Tiptree and Tolleshunt D'arcy. The famous Tiptree Jams are a present day example.

After the Norman Conquest of England, East Anglia and Essex were the areas into which Flemish craftsmen began to settle. Teachers from the Flanders taught local people in Essex their superior methods of weaving. By the beginning of the fifteenth century great improvements were achieved in both the variety and quality of clothes woven. The raw local grown wool was given out mostly to women and children working in their cottages locally. These interesting cottages and houses in Coggeshall are repeated in areas such as Sudbury, Long Melford and at Lavenham in Suffolk.

## THE BUSH FAMILY SAIL ON THE MAYFLOWER

Devoutly religious and ambitious families like the Bushes and the sons of Lawrence Washington fled the religious persecution by the Catholics to Massachusetts and New England in America. All helped and advised by the skipper of the Mayflower who was related to and conducted commodity business with all the local pastoral families. The Bushes for example supplied wheat and foods carried on the Mayflower, and were probably the first pioneers to export seed to the Americas.

# ESSEX WOMEN AND CRAFTSMEN THE BEST

Aside from the religious persecution by the Catholics, the years 1600 - 1650 were periods of 'Land Hunger' exacerbated by a shortage of farm workers. Land rents continued to rise and land for sale or lease was difficult to find. Farm workers were moving out of farming, and into cottage industries were offered shorter hours and better pay.

In contrast, Massachusetts, America offered work for craftsmen in the country where their skills were appreciated. Free land and religious freedom were the greatest prizes of all.

The Master of the Mayflower was astutely aware that his friends from Maldon and the surrounding villages were quite capable of setting up self sufficient and sustaining villages in the American wilderness. The craftsmen could build cottages, barns, furniture, and farm implements.

Essex wives could weave, bake, milk, cook, help with the harvest, make clothes and rear children. All skills necessary for a self-sustaining community, such women would be difficult to find in Essex in modern times.

### NOTE

Catholic King, Charles I (1600 - 49) and his catholic wife continued, with the Roman church to torture and murder any Protestants and Puritans in and around Essex and London who would not renounce their non-catholic faith. Three hundred who refused to renounce their faith were burnt at the stake. This cruelty continued until Oliver Cromwell and his 'roundheads' brought the persecution and murder by Catholics of non-Catholics to an end.

THE TRUE STORY OF ROBIN HOOD
THE DISPOSSESSED EARL OF HUNTINGDON
WHO CHANGED THE COURSE OF
BATTLEFIELD TACTICS FOREVER.

WILLIAM LORD CLINTON,
EARL OF HUNTINGDON,
LORD ADMIRAL OF ENGLAND AND IRELAND
SUCCEEDED TO THE TITLE OF
EARL OF HUNTINGDON

A STORYTELLER RECOUNTING THE TALES OF
ROBIN HOOD AT A NOTTINGHAM FAIR IN 1295

WILLIAM LORD CLINTON, JUSTICE OF CHESTER, GOVERNOR OF
DOVER CASTLE, WARDEN OF CINQUE PARTS, LORD ADMIRAL OF
ENGLAND – CREATED EARL OF HUNTINGDON

# ROBIN HOOD
# VS
# WILLIAM LORD CLINTON
# EARL OF HUNTINGDON

In 1330, William Lord Clinton, Lord Admiral of England, Justice of Chester, Governor of Dover Castle, Warden of the Cinque Ports, was appointed to the title of Earl of Huntingdon, filling the title once held by Anglo Saxon Robin Hood. (Robert Ootheur) before he was dispossessed of his title by the Normans.

In 1338 William Clinton, Earl of Huntingdon, was appointed to guard the seashores of all land in Kent where ships plied their trade.

There is no doubting that William Clinton; Earl of Huntingdon was a brave and outstanding military leader. One famous incident recorded in 1340 involved a Norman Ship, "James of Dieppe" which sailed stealthily into the English Port of Sandwich. The Norman crew then set about stealing an English ship by trying to drag it from its moorings. Unfortunately for the Normans, Earl Clinton was on board. Although outnumbered, Earl Clinton and his sailors fought off the Norman attack and turned the tails on them by capturing the "James of Dieppe" with many dead on board.

# ROBIN HOOD

**The Archer who changed the course of English battlefield tactics for centuries.**

Tales about Robin Hood are gems of romance that have been around for over seven hundred years, and enjoyed by millions of readers around the world. However, Robin Hood's real value in English History has never been told. Readers knew Robin Hood as a gallant hero, who lived in the great age of English Archery 13th and 15th Century. Expert with the long bow Friend of Kings and Knights, he lived in Sherwood Forest, in the county of Nottingham, England, around the thirteenth century. Some historians describe his real identity as the dispossessed Earl of Huntingdon, Robert Fitz Ootheur.

# The Real Robin Hood

None of the ancient poems or songs or early-published information however, record Robin Hood's real and important contribution to English History. That his knowledge of the longbow and what it could achieve using intelligent design of different arrowheads for use in warfare, changed the course of battlefield tactics for centuries, following his friendship with King Edward I.

Robin Hood is not a myth, as some would have us believe. He was in fact very real and lived in a period of experiment and development of the long bow (13th to 15th Centuries). The long bow became a powerful weapon that could change the course of a battle.

Robin Hood lived in Sherwood Forest, Nottingham, with a band of outlaws. An outlaw was anyone who failed to appear before a Court to answer a transgression of the law. Once a Court pronounced a judgment of outlawry, the outlaw concerned could be lawfully killed by anyone who chose to do the deed. The forest was the only hiding place, an area of refuge for such people. Many of Robin's men were professionally trained archers escaping unwilling conscripted service because their Captain had not paid them. It was not unusual for a ruthless Captain to pocket men's pay, which he would explain away to his Lord as a precaution, to deprive those of money who he suspected were saving to pay a fine to a local Court; to be released from the conscripted service for which they had signed up.

Most of the main characters surrounding the stories of Robin Hood dressed in Lincoln Green, with the exception of Friar Tuck, a bawdy, overweight drunken Monk. Another was Will Scarlet; he was a good all rounder with longbow, sword, fighting staff and wrestling skills. Lastly was a man known as Little John, seven foot tall, who was said to be able to crack open a mans skull with one blow of his two meter long oak staff. Robin Hood himself was a man of honour, courteous and generous. He wins every battle against corruption and evil.

Robin Hood is also said to be more devout to the disciplines of Holy Mary than Friar Tuck. He was a man who was unafraid of Knight or Sheriff. In a time of Lawlessness in England, he improved the lot of those around him. He stands for justice and against corrupt sheriff officials. On the social side of his life, every cause for celebration becomes a feast with food and drinks a plenty for everyone. No one was excluded from King to nobleman, to Knight to the kitchen maid. Robin Hood has all the attributes of any modern day hero who gives hope to the down trodden and sucker to the poor.

Ranged against Robin and his men on the opposite side of the official divide in those desperate times, were the corrupt local officials who were not beyond bribery, kidnap, extortion and even murder for money.

## AUTHOR'S NOTES

Following his victory at the Battle of Hastings, William the Conqueror, dispossessed around 4000 Anglo Saxon families of their titles, land and property, which he distributed to a mere 1000 Norman barons.

Robin Hood is said to be William Fitz Ootheur, the dispossessed Anglo Saxon Earl of Huntingdon. Reduced to being a commoner, the accomplished Earl vowed to continue Anglo Saxon resistance to the Norman overlords taking refuge in Sherwood Forest where workers joined him from his former estate, and others on the run from the Courts or the sheriff's men. All were looking for a natural leader who would help them survive in the forest by poaching the Kings deer, when they could earn as much money in two weeks equal to labouring one year on a farm.

Robin Hood claimed not to rob the rich travellers or merchants travelling to Nottingham or beyond, but to be charging a toll to anyone travelling through any part of the forest Robin and his men controlled. Much of the money and goods gained by Robin's men were given to the poor. The whole story of Robin Hood and his men gives a feel of continued resistance by Anglo Saxons to the Norman takeover.

# THE LONGBOW

There are differing accounts and opinions about the date in history accorded to Robin Hood and his merry men. It is probable that for nearly two centuries there were several families of outlaws whose antics were attributed to Robin Hood and his men. Most of the stories have come down to us in ballads. plays and poetry performed by travelling minstrels and storytellers. Written accounts did not appear until 1375. It is, however, acceptable to assume some dates from clues left by other events of those times, including Robin's friendship with Edward I of England. For example, Robin Hood was famous for his expertise and exploits with the longbow.

The longbow, however, was not re-invented in England until 1250-75 in the reign of Edward I. The weapon came into common use in England by the yeoman from the Midland forests. Who in turn learned how to make and master the use of the longbow from the Welsh hill men close to the Welsh borders who developed the bow during the welsh wars against Edward I.

The bow was known as the longbow of Gwent, an area famous for its fine archers, many of who would later join the army of Edward I as mercenaries on his expedition into Scotland.

The Welsh bow was carved from a piece of rough unpolished elm. English Archers operating in the wooded lands of Shropshire, Macclesfield, Sherwood, developed a longer, heavier, superior bow from a stave of yew. The English bow was more flexible and less likely to snap in two above the handhold. Beeswax was used on the flax stringing which gave the bow more power from a taught pull. Their arrow shafts were often made from oak, tipped with a long steel arrowhead that could pierce chain mail and plate Armour at 250 paces.

AN EARLY CROSSBOW WITH BOLTS IN A
SHORT POUCH ON THE WAIST

THE GWENT BOW MUCH INFERIOR TO THE ENGLISH LONGBOW

A POPINJAY MAKER AT KENTWELL HALL IN SUFFOLK.
POPINJAY – ORGIN FRENCH. A STUFFED TARGET IN THE SHAPE
OF A BIRD FOR ARCHERY PRACTICE.

Robin Hood and his men had a major military advantage over the Sheriff of Nottingham. Robin Hood's men were able to produce their own weaponry from an endless supply of materials in the forest. A 'bowyer' would fashion the staves of wood from the best materials in the forest for the longbows, which stood 1.8 meters (6ft). The 'Fletcher' made Arrows in large numbers from a large choice of branches on the trees. The stringing was made by the 'string fellow'. The 'arrow smith' made various styles of arrowheads.

The longbow could be fired at any angle, and arrows could fire 300 yards in rapid succession with different heads to pierce chain mail, plate armour or horse armour.

Ranged against Robin Hood and his men were well-armed Sheriffs men with crossbows - a weapon that could fire in a straight line for 125 paces but lost momentum if fired at an angle. Reloading after firing each bolt took longer than loosing arrows. No match for the skilled longbow archers using rapid fire. The sheriff's men would be wearing helmets of steel and padded jackets. Robin's men did not have the quilted gambeson jacket or steel helmets because they were well protected by the maze of trees between them and a bolt fired from a straight fire crossbow.

ENGLISH ARROWS THAT COULD PIERCE
CHAINMAIL, PLATE ARMOUR, AND HORSE
ARROWS; THAT BROUGHT ENGLISH VICTORIES
ON FRENCH BATTLEFIELDS FOR TWO CENTURIES.

ARROW HEADS BASED ON DESIGNS BY ROBIN HOOD FOR KING EDWARD I FOR MILITARY USE IN SCOTLAND.

The English longbow used with arrowheads designed specifically to be effective in knocking out different targets on a battlefield, was to prove vitally important to success in future battlefield warfare. It was Robin Hood who brought this developed strategy to the attention of the King, who was planning an expedition into Scotland - a brave and capable King who had survived a Crusade to the Holy Land. The English longbow was to become a most feared weapon. Feared particularly by the French. Skilled longbow men could fire off fifteen arrows in one minute that would fly straight to the target with a now outstanding accuracy. At the end of a day's battle, archer's fingers would bleed from their efforts. Archers would plunge their arrowheads into dirty ground before firing so that wounds inflicted by arrows would become infected.

A tactic known as a 'clout' was developed for use on the battlefield when literally a cloud of arrows would be fired high into the air so that they would gain both speed and momentum when falling onto the enemy.

Trained and disciplined longbow archers used by Edward III brought a victory against overwhelming odds of more than three to one in the battle of Crecy, France in 1346, fighting French mounted Knights clad in plate armour. England's sturdy yeoman with longbow, now wearing steel helmets, chain mail and gambesons were in the first rank of all English armies. English commanders would order their archers to fire showers or a 'clout' of arrows with different steelheads that neither man nor horse could pass through without being injured. Consequently the punishment meted out to archers taken prisoner was to have the first three fingers of their bow pulling hand cut off.

ONE OF THE COUNTRY'S TOP MASTER SMITHS
AT KENTWELL HALL IN SUFFOLK,

FIRE ARROWS WOULD BE SOAKED IN PITCH TO ENSURE THEY BLAZED

ARROW MAKING BY WOMENFOLK

ARROW MAKING BY WOMENFOLK

ENGLISH LONGBOWMEN CONFIDENT IN THE POWER
AND RELIABILITY OF THEIR LONGBOW

GWENT MERCINARIES ADMIRING THE ENGLISH LONGBOW

# AUTHORS NOTES

Lord "Rayner the Flemming", and his sons, and their descendants retained the trust and respect of the Norman Royalty for centuries. They continued their duties of transferring taxes and valuables from the Midlands and the North, including Nottingham Castle, to the Kings Keep in Colchester and Winchester.

The original Rayner the Flemming, nicknamed the 'Mighty Warrior', grew close to Eudo Daphier, Steward to William the Conqueror and Lord of Colchester, who built Colchester Keep for William the Conqueror. Eudo gave the hand of more than one of his daughters in marriage to Rayner's sons. The title 'Lord of Colchester' is now the entitlement of the Author being the oldest of his surviving line of his family. Arrows bore the colour or mark of the archer who fired the arrow. The chattels and goods on a dead body pierced by an arrow belonged to the archer who fired that arrow. At Crecy, many English archers died fighting each other in disputes over whose arrow was the first to kill the enemy.

Robin Hood taught King Edward that archers could be used to devastating effect by using the right arrowheads for the task to be undertaken. Fire arrows, for example, were hammered and formed so that they enclosed a ball of cotton, or a shape where a length of cotton could be threaded through and round the head. The cotton tied head was then soaked in oil and pitch, set alight, and fired into wooden works or haystacks. Armour piercing heads were heavy pyramid shape. These heads would vibrate on striking metal plate armour, which helped the head pierce its way through the metal. They had long thin shaped heads for piercing chain mailarge barbed heads for piercing a horse's coat. By the fifteenth century, there were at least 18 different shaped arrowheads in use. One arrowhead shaped like a crescent moon at right angles could pierce armour and cut through the ribs of the enemy.

ARCHERY PRACTICE BECOMES LAW FOR EVERYONE

ARCHERY PRACTICE BECOMES LAW FOR EVERYONE

The King was so impressed with the longbow he made it compulsory for every male between the ages of 16-60 to own and practice the skill of the longbow. Practice on Sundays became compulsory and every village green was the height of activity with wives and families joining in the fun. The longbow was not given up by the army as an official weapon of war until the 19th century.

Much of the information about the various arrowheads was confirmed when the well preserved artifacts from Henry VIII's flagship the 'Mary Rose' which sank in 1545 in Portsmouth Harbour while sailing into battle, were recovered by divers and placed on display in Portsmouth, England.

Robin Hood was a devout Catholic, who liked to attend confession, and is said to have lived without wife or children. Robin Hood always wore a hood or a hat on his head, probably in respect to 'Our Lady'. Although most archers wore felt hats in those time against fleas and lice.

Each year when the seasonal fairs came round in spring and summer, Robin Hood accompanied by Friar Tuck and Little John would ride twenty miles or more from the far reaches of Sherwood to compete in the games at Barnsdale, for example where they would meet up with Will Scarlet who was always a keen competitor. Robin and his men would barter or sell the finest bows and arrows to obtain thread for their 'fletcher', and other goods needed in their forest hide out. Robin was also a master of disguises, and would compete as a visiting yeoman in archery, sword and wrestling contests, where he was a frequent winner of prizes, which he would give away to locals.

These events were often watched by the King and his entourage, it was common for villages to hold archery competitions on Sundays after church or practice in the main village street to the peril of passers by, in preparation for the archery competitions on feast days and public holidays. There is a story that at Whitby, famous for its 'jet jewellery,' there were two pillars of stone a kilometer apart, set up to commemorate Robin Hoods mastery of the longbow.

ARCHERS IN CAMP AT A COUNTY LONG BOW SPEED
COMPETITION, WHICH WAS WON BY A WOMAN

ARCHERS IN CAMP AT A COUNTY LONG BOW SPEED
COMPETITION, WHICH WAS WON BY A WOMAN

## NOTES

Most of the place names associated with Robin Hood are in Nottingham; hence he was known as Robin of Nottingham. William the Conqueror had an illegitimate son, William Peverel, to whom he gave over 100 Lordships in and around Nottingham, and created him Earl of Nottingham. William Peverel built Nottingham Castle in 1068 and was the first Sheriff of Nottingham. His son also called William inherited his father's wealth; and was also Sheriff of Nottingham.

## THE NORMAN SHERRIFF OF NOTTINGHAM

The Sheriff of Nottingham in the days of Robin Hood had more problems than most with the highwaymen. Some of whom had been at large in the forest for 20 years. Made possible because there was no love lost between the Saxons who worked the field and lived near or in the forests, and the corrupt Norman Sheriffs or Norman King's officials. The Saxon people were sympathetic to both Highwaymen and Outlaws alike and would warn Robin Hood and his men when the Kings troop were lying in wait in the forest or when the Sheriffs men had set up a trap or ambush. King Edward, a capable warrior in his own right was said to be an admirer of Robin Hood and his skill with the longbow and the skilled use of different arrows.

King Edward saw the potential of the longbow as a military weapon. King Edward also admired Robin's ability with the sword, and his wrestling ability at local fairs and Games, which the King would sometimes attend. King Edward is said to have visited with Robin Hood in Sherwood to learn more about the deadly longbow and arrows; discuss methods he could adopt to train his troops to use the bow in a disciplined way during his planned expeditions with his army into Scotland. It is said, however that the Sheriff of Nottingham never forgave Robin for the taunts he endured from the Kings table for being unable to capture Robin Hood and his men. The Sheriff was said to have been aware that the King knew exactly where to find Robin and his men in the forest, but kept silent, and even tipped off Robin before raids by the Sheriffs men because he needed Robins expertise.

Robin and his band continued to rob the Manorial Lords, wealthy Abbots, and Courtly Officials and wine and wool merchants travelling through Sherwood to deliver the Kings taxes to the sheriff of Nottingham at Nottingham Castle. The Sheriff would respond by stepping up patrols into the forest, and sending expeditions of troops to capture Robin and his men, but without result. When the sheriff's troops entered the forest as many as 50-100 archers would emerge from the trees and fire salvos of arrows at the Sheriffs troops; arrows that could pierce chain mail and bring down horses. The sheriff's men would quickly retreat, whilst Robin Hood's men would melt away disguised by their Lincoln Green, into the forest.

## THE GAME OF NOUGHTS AND CROSSES

English military supremacy in archery was accepted throughout Europe, a fact established at Agincourt, Crecy and Poitiers.

The secrets of the English success was the six foot long bow which was bent and powerful to over 300 paces, and although it was a difficult weapon to use, requiring whole body strength, the English were deft at operating the bow from a young age when practice was compulsory. Early arrow pouches used by Robin Hood's men were woven from cane with nine square spacer holes at the mouth, to stop arrow goose feathers from losing their shape. The nine square holes are said to be the basis of the ancient game of noughts and crosses. A late development by military archers was a spacer made from a piece of thick leather drilled with twelve holes for use when combining rapid fire of twelve arrows every minute.

## KNIGHT RAYNER THE FLEMMING AND ROBIN HOOD

The author's ancestor, Lord Rayner the Flemming, under Earl Warenne, founded and endowed a small Priory at Kirklees. Lord Rayner's relative, a Cistercian nun, was installed at the Abbey to keep a close eye on the running of the Priory, and to offer frequent prayers for the well being of the Rayner family.

The Abbess was a cousin of Robin Hood and Robin made frequent visits to Kirklees taking money for the upkeep of the Priory. Kirklees was also a safe haven for Robin when he was away from the protection of the forest and his men.

## ARCHERY SPEED CONTEST

A woman archer who loosed 19 arrows in one minute won an archery speed contest with archers competing from all over the County of Essex. The male runner up loosed 14 arrows. Observing the best of the archers it was noticeable that when one arrow was hitting the target, the second arrow was in the air as the third was being offered to the bow. On the battlefield 20 English archers could loose 500 armour-piercing arrows in a minute towards oncoming cavalry.

In France, it is claimed that during the battle of Crecy an arrow pierced a knight's right thigh, went through the horse and into his left leg, pinning him into his saddle.

## THE DEATH OF ROBIN HOOD

In the end Robin Hood is said to have died by treachery. The stories tell how Robin Hood rode to Kirklees Priory near Wakefield, to have his blood let by the Prioress, who was allegedly his cousin. Blood letting by cut artery or leaches was common practice in those times, thought to cure any malady. Robin Hood died at the priory. It is said that the Prioress was in love with a nobleman close to the sheriff of Nottingham, and that she poisoned Robin for the reward; prayed for his soul and took the money. In the authors opinion it is equally possible that if we take the romance out from the story, Robin Hood died of blood poisoning contracted whilst having his blood let. Research shows that the Priory was still functioning in the fourteenth century when it was reproved by the Catholic Bishop for disobedience, which may mean it became a house of ill repute.

### NOTES

Rayner the Flemmings were Crusader Knights, trusted by William the Conqueror, and fought on his right flank at Hastings. Eudo Daphier, steward to William the Conqueror was given Colchester in Essex, and the title of Lord of Colchester in the Norman Settlement.

# COLCHESTER CASTLE
## BIGGEST 'KEEP' IN WILLIAM THE CONQUERER'S ENGLAND

A THIEF IN THE STOCKS AT COLCHESTER IN 1845

Eudo, a trusted aid to King William built upon the site of a Roman Castle, and Saxon Fort in Colchester, and turned it into a Royal Stronghold, with a 'Keep' bigger that any other Norman Keep in England. Eudo also endowed an Abbey on the South side of the town.

Crusader Knight, Knight Templar, Rayner the Flemming transferred taxes from Wakefield and Nottingham to Eudo Daphier in Colchester. Sons and daughters from both families intermarried. Eudo Daphiers descendants inherited title and lands in the Midlands. Eudo Daphiers great grandson William Fitz Ootheur is said to be a claimant to the Earldom of Huntingdon in the middle of the twelfth century.

Dr William Stukeley, a Lincolnshire Antiquary, fellow of the Society of Antiquarians claimed that Robert Fitz Ootheur was the original Robin Hood.

Most of the early ballads about Robin Hood paint a picture of a devout man, who attended church and confession regularly, praying through Holy Mary. He appeared to have little room in his life for women. Both Robin Hood and Little John were said to have been captured eventually by the Sheriffs men. However both men received the Kings pardon for their misdeeds.

We do not know if there is any truth in this claim because most of the stories handed down over the centuries have had their contents altered. Although taking into account the fact that Robin Hood did help King Edward, and worked with him for a time to introduce the longbow and arrowheads into military use, a Kings pardon would not be unusual.

New characters were made up and introduced into many of the original tales to please the changing political tastes of theatre audiences of the day. Most of the original tales, although strange to our thinking were simple and straightforward, and have a ring of truth about them. Here is one of the well-known examples of the earliest stories

# THE POTTERS TALE

Little John accosted a potter travelling with his wares through Sherwood Forest towards Barnsdale, and demanded that the potter, known as Percy the Potter, pay a toll. Percy refused, and after a fracas in which Little John was coming off second best, John retreated gracefully into the forest.

John knew that the potter travelled regularly with his wares to the market at Barnsdale. John decided that the only way to test the potters fighting ability fully was to get him to fight Robin Hood. Little John challenged Robin with a wager that he, Robin Hood, would fail in any attempt to make Percy the Potter pay a toll for passing through the forest territory towards Barnsdale.

Robin enjoyed rising to Johns challenge; stopped the Potter and demanded that the Potter pay a toll. The Potter refuses, and the pair fought, Robin with the sword, and the Potter with his oak staff. Unusually, the Potters skill with his staff gets the better of Robin, knocking the sword from Robin's hand the Potter pins Robin to the ground with his staff. The Potter then gives Robin a lecture on the error of his ways. That it is wrong for a devout man of Robins reputation to charge strangers a toll to pass through the forest that Robin does not own, but is in fact the property of the King.

Robin can find no fault in the Potters argument, but points out the difficulties under which he and his men live, by opposing the wicked Norman Sheriff of Nottingham and protecting the poor from the injustice metered out by their Norman overlords, and their corrupt officials and courts. Robin suggests to the Potter that the only way he can experience the difficulties under which he and his men live under Norman domination is to exchange clothes. The Potter readily agrees, and they exchange clothes, with Robin agreeing that dressed as a Potter he will sell the Potters wares.

Robin keeps his word and successfully sells the Potters wares on his way through the forest to Nottingham. Robin has only a few more expensive pieces left when he is surprised by the appearance of the wife of the Sheriff of Nottingham riding out with her ladies in waiting. The Sheriffs wife enquires about his wares and Robin presents her with his most expensive pieces. She is best pleased and invites Robin (the Potter) to dinner at the Castle to receive payment for his wares from her husband the Sheriff.

During dinner at the castle the Sheriff talks about an upcoming archery contest between villagers and the Sheriffs men below the castle walls. Robin (the Potter) expresses his interest in taking part in the contest, hence the Sheriff orders the Master at Arms to provide Robin with a longbow of his choice and a pouch of arrows. The Potter excels in the archery contest, and the Sheriff is keen to know where the Potter acquired his archery skills. The Potter informs the Sheriff that he knows Robin Hood personally from selling his wares to villages in the forest. He also has a bow made by Robin Hood in his cart in the forest, which he uses to practice under Robin Hoods favourite oak tree. On the following morning the Sheriff and his party decide to accompany the Potter to his favourite spot in Sherwood; to try his bow, and perhaps meet Robin Hood in person, who he secretly plans to arrest by ordering his Master at Arms to follow their trail with his best men.

On reaching the forest, the pretend Potter sounds his horn and two hundred archers in the Lincoln Green appear from nowhere to greet their leader. The Master at Arms and his men seeing themselves greatly outnumbered by skilled longbow men, flee back to the castle leaving the Sheriff and his party to their fate.

Robin decides to help himself to the Sheriffs fine horse, much to the amusement of the Sheriffs wife who is allowed to keep hers, and send the Sheriff unharmed on his way on foot. Robin sets up a feast of roasted venison and ale for the Potter, and his men, and the villagers; pays the real potter for his wares and they part good friends, with the promise to the Potter that he may travel without paying a toll anywhere in Sherwood forest and beyond to village fairs.

# TOPOGRAPHY

Nottingham and Sherwood Forest in Nottingham have remained the centres of the cult of Robin Hood. Nottingham was a county town. Barnsdale, which features in some of the stories was a Wayside Halt. Kirklees Convent was endowed by Lord Rayner and his family (the writers ancestors).

Robin Hood almost certainly lived around 1190-1274. His tales are entertaining; he is against the wealthy lording it over the poor; he cocks a snoot at the Royal Forest Law, corrupt Sheriffs and government officials. And in spite of being said to be a pleasure seeker and robber, he reveres Holy Mary and the King. He is one of histories lovable rascals.

# THE THREE EDWARDS 1272-1377

**KING EDWARD I** stayed at Nottingham Castle, resting on his campaigns with his army to and from Scotland.

**KING EDWARD II** held Court in Nottingham Castle, and in 1337, a Parliament was again held in Nottingham.

**KING EDWARD III** the youthful King entered Nottingham Castle through a secret passage. He was accompanied by castle guards to help him arrest the hated Roger de Mortimer, who became his mother's lover shortly after the death of his father. The youthful King confronted Roger de Mortimer. A brief fight ensued in which two of Mortimers bodyguards died. The brave young Edward took Mortimer to the Tower of London. He was hanged at the London gallows known as the Tyburn Tree. Queen Isabella was kept a prisoner in Nottingham Castle for many years before being confined to a Nunnery.

### NOTES

All three Edwards 1272-1377 were very capable fighting men. Able to hold their own in contests and competitions at village and County Fairs. Of the three King Edwards, Edward I was the only Crusader King.

# ANCIENT BACKGROUND HISTORY

In the days of Robin Hood, Nottingham Forest was 25 miles in length and ten miles wide; was the property of the King, and governed by Forest laws, which were oppressive and very strictly enforced by the sheriff.

Blidworth - Will Scarlet is said to be buried in an ancient cemetery. A cave under the village is said to be the store place of the outlaws food and possessions.

Fountain Dalo - Friar Tuck is said to have lived in Harlow Wood.

Clipstone - Road to Mansfield. Once stood an ancient oak named Parliament oak, where King Edward I held parliament. It was also a favourite tree of King John.

Edwinstone - Said to be the gateway to the paths Robin Hood and his merry men frequented, leading to the greatest oaks in the forest; Queen Oak, and Robin Hoods Larder. Queen Oaks a gigantic tree 1000 years old grows in Birland Wood.

Papplewick - Robin Hood said to have stabled his horses in a cave.

# A PERSONAL VIEW OF THE BATTLE OF HASTINGS IN 1066

KING HAROLD'S MEN SETTING UP CAMP AFTER A FORCED MARCH TO HASTINGS ON ENGLAND'S SOUTH COAST

RELIGIOSE BLESSING THE CAMP

# VIKINGS TURNED NORMANS
## DUKE WILLIAM OF NORMANDY, FRANCE

Normandy is a Province on the north coast of France, with the River Seine at its centre. The King of France in return for the cessation of raids and hostilities, and a promise to help defend France against other Viking groups gave up the Province to the Vikings leader Rollo. (The name Norman comes from the name north-men, the ancient name for Vikings) The Vikings, turned Normans, adopted the French language and Christian religion and became indistinguishable from the native French.

Duke William of Normandy was the illegitimate son of Duke Robert I, William was born in Falaise, Normandy where his bronze figure, lance in hand on a spirited horse stands in the square today, guarding the approach to his ducal castle. His mother was his father's mistress Herleve - Arlette the daughter of the towns Tanner, Fulbert. Williams father, Duke Robert spotted Herleve-Arlette from a window in the castle and William was the fruit of their union. His mother later married a Viscount, and had two sons - Bishop Odo, and Count Robert of Montain, Williams half brothers who were to play important roles at Hastings and in ruling England.

Duke Robert joined other prominent Normans, such as Tancred, and Eustace of Boulogne on a Pilgrimage to the Holy Land. Before leaving on the fatal unofficial crusade Robert decided to designate his illegitimate son William, to be his heir upon his death.
Although Duke Robert was a candidate for the job of Patriarch of Jerusalem, Robert wanted to return home, probably due to the constant factional squabbling over who should hold the important positions in Jerusalem. Tragically Duke Robert was killed returning home from Asia Minor, and his illegitimate son William, duly took the ducal crown at the age of seven years in 1035.

## DUKE WILLIAM OF NORMANDY

William grew into a strong, tall, but not ungainly fierce Knight, and would often be seen riding with a hawk on his fist. It is written that 'No Knight in France was his equal when it came to fighting and leading men into battle'. Battles took place almost every year. Battles in which William triumphed.

William was known to be vindictive. This was borne out when William refused a grave to the bodies of King Harold and his two Brothers at Hastings.

A SCRIBE KEEPING RECORDS

A MONEYER STRIKING COINS FOR KING EDWARD I

THE BISHOP OF BURY ST. EDMONDS, SUFFOLK ENGLAND
WITH THE CLERK TO THE KING

# ENGLAND'S EDWARD THE CONFESSOR
## 1049-1065

On this side of the English Channel reigned King Edward the Confessor. Edwards mother was Norman, consequently Edward was brought up and educated in Normandy. It is the writers opinion that Edward was more French than English. A pious man, he spent most of his days hunting, and in devotion to God. In 1049, Edward was occupied building Westminster Abbey, which was completed in 1065. The day to day running of England in the meantime was managed by Earl Harold of Wessex, Edwards brother-in-law, both men being of Viking descent. In order to be close to his Westminster Abbey project on which he devoted much of his time and money, King Edward moved the Royal Residence from the walled City of London, to the Palace of Westminster.

King Edward died unexpectedly on January 5th 1066, without issue, shortly after the consecration of Westminster Abbey on the 28th December. A comet illuminated the sky above his deathbed and King Edward prophesied that a time of evil was coming to England.

There were four claimants to the English throne: The two brothers of the Queen, Tostig Earl of Northumbria until 1065, before being dispossessed by Edward. Harold Godwinson, Earl of Wessex. Harold Haadraada III King of Norway. The fourth and strongest claimant was William, Duke of Normandy. Both he and the deceased King were directly descended form Richard I, Duke of Normandy.

However, on the day following the King Edwards death, the Witan Egemot - the assembly of Saxon Nobles, declared Earl Harold of Wessex, King of England.

# ENGLAND'S KING HAROLD

When news reached Duke William of Normandy Edwards cousin, that Harold had accepted the Crown of England, William was outraged because Edward the Confessor had sent Harold to William in Normandy to inform him that he, Duke William would be the next King of England. Duke William made Harold swear an oath on his Holy Relics he wore around his neck, and the Relics in the Church; that Harold would respect William's entitlement to the Crown of England. William sent formal messengers to Harold in England demanding that King Harold renounce the crown in Williams favour, and honour his oath sworn on Holy relics. When King Harold rebuffed both messengers, William decided to act; to seize the English throne by force of arms, and punish Harold for breaking his oath: an act of perjury in those times.

AN APOTHECARY WAITING TO ATTEND THE WOUNDED

## NOTES - HOLY RELICS

Solemn oaths in medieval times were not sworn on the Bible because it was not available in printed form until 1625 (the first handwritten version 1382). Instead solemn oaths were sworn on Holy Relics, and to break an oath so sworn was a very serious matter indeed. Personal Holy Relics may consist of anything from a piece of the true cross; an alleged thorn from the Crown of Thorns worn by Jesus at his Crucifixion; a saints fingernail, or a piece of wool woven by Holy Mary and so on.

In the absence of the Bible, relics were the focal point for peoples beliefs. All revered Holy Relics, which were thought to possess miraculous powers. Something people could touch and feel Gods power. There were also public relics on which an oath could be sworn stored in local churches. Relics such as an arm or body, said to be that of a Saint.

William the Conqueror or Duke William was a devout Catholic. His personal relics hung about his neck and are likely to have been in the form of a heavy cast gold crucifix with Christ on the cross. The crucifix will have been in two parts, held together with gold wire or a hinge to contain a sacred Holy Relic. The heavy crucifix probably hung on a string of patterned heads of white and yellow amber, coral, jet and precious stones possibly decorated

with hand carvings. This item would have been very important and precious to William, and an oath sworn upon it considered to be unbreakable.
Relics in his Church were the bodies of two martyrs set in the Alter, on which Harold was said to have sworn the oath, 'that he Duke William would be the next King of England'. An oath that was binding and irrevocable.

# DUKE WILLIAMS PLAN TO BECOME KING OF ENGLAND

Williams plan to legitimize the seizure of the Crown of England was both clever and cunning. William set out to gain the full support of the Pope by sending a delegation to witness King Harold's broken oaths and consequent blasphemy. Also to point out to the Pontiff that he, William would return English worshippers to the Catholic Church thereby adding a second papal fief.

The Pope gave the full backing of the Church in Rome to Williams claim, that he William was the rightful heir to the English throne. The Pope also gave William a specially consecrated banner to be carried into battle by a chosen knight. William thus succeeded in turning his claim to the Crown of England into a Crusade under the Papal aegis of returning England to the Church.

A Crusade was something European Knights and mercenaries understood. Particularly when there were the prospects of land, loot and titles to be had, all much closer to home than pilgrimages to the Middle East. Most Knights enlisted purely for the plunder.

Knights with trained forces flocked to William's cause from all over Europe; Brittany, Flanders, Aquitaine and Italy. The success of Williams appeal left him with the mammoth task of putting together a massive fleet of 700 flat-bottomed ships in which to carry an army of eight thousand. Comprising Knights, fighting men, horses and supplies from Dives in France, to Pevensey Bay on England's South Coast. The ships posed a major challenge, together with assembling sufficient number of horses. The whole project must have been a logistical nightmare, not to mention feeding and disciplining such a large force until the invasion set sail for England. The rest is well known history and sets the rise and rise of the Clintons.

# VIKING DIVERSIONARY ATTACK ON YORK

Baldwin, Duke William's father-in-law was a close friend of Tostig, King Harold's dispossessed younger brother. Tostig was also a close friend of King Harold Haadraada; exiled himself at one time, also a claimant to the English throne, promised to help Tostig regain his title and lands in England, which King Harold had taken away from Tostig for ill-treating his people.

It is very obvious that Duke William of Normandy persuaded and encouraged Tostig and Haadraada to launch an invasion on the north of England to draw King Harold and his army away from the South, around the time William was expecting to land his invasion force in Pevensey Bay. Also to prevent the Northern Earls rushing to London to support Harold, fulfilling the role of Harold's reinforcements. To gain King Harold's attention Tostig's small fleet attacked and sacked villages along the North Sea Coast of England en route to meetings up with King Haadraadas fleet as prearranged. Both men then set sail into the river Humber with between two and three hundred long ships. Open boats about 70ft in length, and rowed by thirty Vikings, each long ship carrying around 50 to 60 fighting men.

Haadraada disembarked at Ricall, around ten miles from the City of York. Harold Haadraada's plan was to take York without destroying the city because it would be Harold's brother Tostig's seat of Government.

# THE VIKINGS WIN YORK

Defending York were the northern Earl brothers Edwin and Morcar, whose sister was married to King Harold. The northern Earls commanded Northumbria and Mercia which encompassed most of the North of England and the Midlands, enabling them to gather together a respectable size force, but hardly a match for hardened Viking mercenaries. The Earls forces filed out of the safety of York towards the village of Fulford to take on the Vikings.

Waiting for them in Fulford were the armies of Harold Haadraada, with Tostig's men on his right. King Harold Haadraada presented a formidable figure. Six foot six inches tall with a frame to match. Tostig was King Harold's younger brother, but was an experienced field commander.

The two armies met. Predictably and in typical Viking fashion, Haadraada and Tostig led counter attack after counter attack on the Earls forces until they gained the upper hand. The two Earls fled with what was left of their armies back to the safety of the walls of York. Pursued by the Vikings the two Earls agreed surrender on humiliating terms, which suited Tostig who wanted to avoid a battle for the City, which was to be his seat of government.

# KING HAROLD FALLS FOR WILLIAM'S PLANNED DIVERSION AND ARRIVES IN YORK TO TAKE ON THE VIKINGS

With York secured, Haadraada and Tostig moved part of their forces out of York to Stamford bridge, eight miles East of York where four roads met at a river crossing. The point where they were expecting English King Harold's army to arrive in about two weeks, the usual travelling time from the South. Confidant they were prepared and guarded against any surprise attack, the Norsemen decided to rest and swim in the hot summer sunshine to recover from the recent victory over the Northern Earls. England's King Harold caught the Vikings completely by surprise; covering 180 miles from the south to Stamford Bridge in just a few days, with a large army outnumbering Haadraadas and Tostig's forces.

The Vikings were further disadvantaged because men had been left to retain control of York, and other forces had been delegated to guard the ships and supplies. Even more important, the Vikings had left much of their chain mail, armour, and heavy shields on the ships, due to the hot weather, and because they did not expect English forces from the south to arrive for at least two weeks.

King Harold, surrounded by his housecarls, probably the best infantry in Europe, crossed the bridge to offer peace terms to the younger brother Tostig, in order to avoid a battle whilst the King was waiting news of movements of the invasion fleet Duke William had built up on the other side of the English Channel. King Harold offered to return Tostig's title, his lands and more. However, Tostig not wishing to betray his sponsors, asked Harold what he would give to Harold Haadraada? The English King replied - "only sufficient soil in which to bury a tall man".

# ENGLAND'S KING HAROLD RECAPTURES YORK

England's King Harold withdrew, and the battle commenced about midday. The lightly dressed and lightly armed Norsemen were no match for the heavily armed, chain mailed housecarls swinging their murderous double handed axes, whilst archers, and sling shots rained down missiles on the lightly clad Vikings without chain mail and battle jerkins to protect themselves. The figure leading the Vikings was King Haadraada who was struck in the throat by an arrow in view of his men and died on the battlefield towards evening. Seeing Haadraadas fate, England's King Harold and his housecarls attacked Tostig his traitorous brother at the Viking centre killing Tostig. With the two Viking leaders killed, and no one to rally a counter attack, the Norsemen realized they were finished and fled back to their ships.

The carnage on the battlefield was such that less than ten per cent of the fleet of 300 Viking ships returned to Norway, leaving King Harold's army to attend their wounded, and celebrate their victory. Yes, England's King Harold gained a decisive victory, but at a cost. He was not to know that the depletion of his housecarls and levies would be a decisive factor in the battle to come. The Vikings lost because they were complacent. They did not have the intelligence available to Duke William and King Harold.
The Vikings were not wearing their leather jerkins and chain mail. Nor did they have their heavy shields and axes with them. What they were probably expecting to face were trained farm boys (fyrd). Instead they faced housecarls, heavily protected, fighting in Roman style, using axes and lances from behind a shield wall.

KING HAROLD'S ARMY RETURNING TO LONDON
AFTER THEIR VICTORY

KING HAROLD'S ARMY RETURNING TO LONDON
AFTER THEIR VICTORY

# While Harold was Away Duke William Lands on England's South Coast

It was obviously part of Williams plan that whilst King Harold was preoccupied with Tostig and Haadraada in the North, William would sail with his invasion fleet from St Valery at the mouth of the Somme on the evening of the 27th September to Pevensey, a small, safe, coastal bay on England's South coast and land unopposed. Pevensey was along from Hastings, and there was an old Roman castle. William's men and horses landed and set about fortifying Pevensey Castle, before moving along the coast to Hastings. At Hastings Duke William's men built a timber fort into which he could retreat and hold if necessary. There was also an excellent harbour, which would enable William to be reinforced with men and supplies from the sea. Landing unopposed had gained William the time he needed to build positions he could defend and hold as long as necessary.

FEEDING KING HAROLDS MEN

NOTES

Duke William had an army of loyal spies in England who helped him choose the best landing site for his invasion fleet. Pevensey Bay was chosen because of its gentle beach, and existence of a Roman Fort with the wall still standing. Generally in good condition on all sides, except the South side where a few repairs were needed. William's men built a fortification within these walls and cleared the bank and ditch.

William also enjoyed the confidence of a handful of highly placed English nobles with Norman connections living in England to whom William wrote letters persuading them that his army was much smaller in size than the force he had originally planned to land on an England's shores.

Duke William knew well that his letters would be regarded as important military intelligence, and would find their way to King Harold by those who would gain favour with the king.

In reality, Duke William's army was bigger than the force of England's King Harold. William's bluff paid off because King Harold was visibly shaken when he saw the size of the Norman army before him, supported by large numbers of Norman archers.

RESTING BEFORE THE BATTLE AHEAD

# ENGLAND'S KING HAROLD PANICS AND RETURNS SOUTH

When messengers reached King Harold near York with the news that Duke William of Normandy had landed near Hastings with a large invasion fleet, Harold marched his tired and depleted forces back to London in a week, leaving behind his unmounted fyrd and archers. After resting in London for a further seven days, King Harold marched his army the sixty miles to Hastings in two days, 11th to the 13th October. However, William had his fifth column of followers in England, watching Harold's movements, and keeping him informed so he would not be taken by surprise by the arrival of King Harold and his army before he was fully prepared for battle.

The grounds of Battle Abbey, six miles north west of Hastings, just south of the town of Battle on the road to Hastings marks the area where the English took up a commanding position. The Normans stood at the Sandy Brook (Senlac in French) on lower ground facing up hill to the English with boggy ground between. King Harold's men were fewer in number than Duke Williams, say 6,000 to 7,500. William also had well supplied archers supporting his Norman, Brettan and Flemish Knights. Three columns of Knights; Norman and Brettans on one side, William commanding the elite at the centre. Flemish commanded by Rayner the Flemming, Italian and French Knights on the other side. King Harold had no divisions of Knights nor Archers. What he did have was his housecarls, the best trained infantry in Europe, based on the Danish Royal Bodyguards, who brought him victory at York.

MAP OF BATTLE PLAN

# KING HAROLD FOOLISH
## TO TAKE ON DUKE WILLIAM

King Harold now had sufficient experience as a general to be aware that with no cavalry or archers he would have to start the battle from a defensive position fighting on foot. Whilst choosing the high ground would help, it was rather impetuous of the English King Harold to decide to go into battle against the most experienced groups of battle hardy Knights in Europe, before waiting for reinforcements to arrive. Nevertheless,

King Harold stood proudly with his banners and his chain mailed housecarls with the foot wide axe blades on two metre staves behind his shield wall with the dragon of Wessex banner unfurled. Brothers, Earl Leofwine and Gyrth were on either flank at point.

## THE BATTLE BEGINS

Bishop Odo took communion with William before the battle. Bishop Odo mounted his white charger, mace in hand, for it was forbidden for him to stab a man. The Gonfalon sent by the Pope was held by Atz - Ron Le Blanc.

Duke William rode into battle wearing the relics (upon which King Harold had sworn his oath) around his neck, confident he could beat Harold. Half brothers Odo, Bishop of Bayeaux with battle mace at the ready riding his famous white horse, and half brother Robert of Mortain on either side. Rayner the Fleming (author's ancestor) stood ahead of the Flemish Knights. The future William Clinton headed the French Knights. Rayner fought under his noble William de Warenne, the elder, who was to marry William's daughter and add his chequers to the Royals. In a battle that lasted a whole day William opened with his Archers. The Archers gave way to the battle seasoned French infantry, standing toe to toe and cheek by joule against the housecarls neither giving away.

The infantry then fell back to allow the fearsome cavalry through. In typical French fashion the Bretton Knights feigned a retreat, enticing the Saxons to leave their wall and then pursue them. A small body of Saxons did charge down the slope, and were rounded on by the French cavalry, and slaughtered. The first hole in the shield wall appears. Nevertheless, the housecarls fought on bravely and the Saxon centre repulsing the Flemish cavalry charges. The cavalry was fighting up hill and on soggy ground, and William was unseated but pushed back his helmet and shouted "look at me well, I am still, and by the grace of God I will be glorious." William remounted waving his helmet and rallying his troops for yet another counter attack. The Knights on the opposite flank to the Brettons feigned their retreat again bringing the Saxon's out of position in the shield wall to whom they dealt with a swift death.

## WILLIAM'S TACTICS WEAR DOWN THE ENGLISH SHIELD WALL

Inevitably gaps began to appear in the Saxon lines because Harold did not have re-enforcements or reserves. William seeing gaps in the shield wall called in reserves and started an assault. He ordered his archers to empty their barrows and pouches and to aim high to fall upon the Saxon lines. The cavalry and infantry were ordered to get onto the ridge and break the Saxon wall.

Duke William would have been aware that the longer the battle lasted the more likely the battle would swing in favour of his seasoned battle hardy troops. All of whom had riches to gain if they prevailed, or a race from death to their fortified position at Hastings and Pevensey if they failed.

## DUKE WILLIAM CLOSES ON HAROLD FOR THE KILL

Suddenly, the battle was lost irretrievably for the English when King Harold standing in the centre of his housecarls on his hilltop position was struck in the eye by an arrow. Seeing what happened Duke William ordered his archers to empty their barrows and pouches into the enemy and bring the battle to a close.

There was now turmoil at the English centre, William sensed that victory was in his grasp. Using the Knights held in reserve he attacked the English centre killing the housecarls who had fought bravely around King Harold to the last man. Both Harold's brothers were also killed. Rayner the Flemming brought down Harold's brother, as he attacked Duke William who had been unhorsed, and from that moment on, was called by Duke William "Rayner Mighty Warrior".

## KING HAROLD IS KILLED
## DUKE WILLIAM IS VICTORIOUS

The loss of the battle and the death of the royal line had a very deep and lasting effect on the British Isles and its peoples. England would be changed for centuries as it was in Roman times.

England would become part of mainstream medieval Europe, and influenced by the ideas of the Latin world, Churches and monasteries would be reformed, adopting the sacred custom and architecture of France. Oxford and Cambridge were to be founded as centres of learning.

### SUMMARY

King Harold had developed a good battle plan, with a heavy shield wall protected by chained mailed javelin throwers and axe wielders. It took most of the day for the Norman Knights to wear down the shield wall. Nevertheless King Harold was likely to lose. He was foolish to take on Duke William without archers to bring down cavalry, plus re-enforcements to fill in gaps in the shield wall as and when they appeared. Harold should not have fallen for the bait and marched his army to Stamford Bridge to take on Tostig and Haadraada when he was well aware that William was waiting to land on England's shores with a large invasion fleet. That decision together with the plan to take on Duke William at Hastings before he was fully prepared lost England to the Norman French.

# ENGLISH HISTORY CLASSES IGNORE FRENCH DOMINATION AND INFLUENCE

From 1066 and for hundreds of years, England was ruled entirely by the Norman French, a fact that appears to have escaped the attention of many English school history books, and school history lessons.

The majority of the English population were Anglo Saxons who worked on the land, and spoke old English. French domination from the Battle of Hastings onwards affected spelling more than pronunciation. The new aristocracy spoke French, which was used in legal proceedings and administration. Early modern English did not re-establish itself until the fifteenth century. From the Battle of Hastings onwards England was ruled by the French aristocracy, and for all intents and purposes was a virtual province of France for hundreds of years.

# ENGLAND A PROVINCE OF NORMANDY

Personal status before the conquest depended upon ones birthright. The Earl was the overlord. A Knight was a Lord who ruled over hereditary tenants. Tenants social status depended upon the amount of land held.
The majority of the population were peasants. (The lot of the peasants remained unchanged after the conquest). This system had been in place for centuries.

Under Anglo Saxon rule, the Manor or Manor Houses were the centres from which estates were run. Tenants (peasants) cultivated the land under compulsory labour service. The manor house itself was usually the centre of administration with a steward or bailiff ministering the regularities of the Manorial Court, and running the general management of the estate. When the Normans took control a long established system was therefore already in place for their manorialization. Villages remained unchanged, becoming part of the system of government when it suited the crown.

The Norman Conquest wrought much evil upon England, and brought nothing new for the ordinary man. Even the appointments in the Norman church were bought and sold. Most of the ordained clergy were in the church only for what they could gain. Almost the entire government of the church was transferred to Norman hands.

## KING WILLIAM MOVES TO SECURE HIS KINGDOM IN ENGLAND

When Duke William was crowned King of England, there were only nine to ten thousand Normans living in England amongst a native population of one and a half to two million people. William knew that the only way few Normans would keep the English in check was to build a network of strategically placed Castles, Garrisons and Keeps. King William directed his steward Eudo Daphier to build a Garrison at Colchester in Essex. Eudo built a castle over the ruins of the Roman Temple of Claudius, which became Williams largest Keep in Europe. (Essex County Council has made an excellent job of preserving the castle and Roman artifacts). Castles were built in Cambridge, Coventry, Exeter, Huntingdon, Lincoln, Nottingham, Warwick and York. There is also an excellent Keep at Headingham in Essex (which stages medieval events, such as jousts).

It took William a further four to five years to gain some control across England, but he continued to face uprisings against his authority from the Fens, the Welsh Marshes, and in the South West.

King William's most impressive stone Keep was the Tower of London. The Tower looks much the same today as when it was finished in 1078. William's son, William Rufus, Henry I and Henry III added gateways, ramparts and towers making it the strongest Keep in Europe next to Colchester.

# ENGLISH BISHOPS REPLACED BY NORMANS

Wealth was spent building an enormous number of Cathedrals, Churches and Abbeys. Normans replaced most English Bishops, further entrenching England's link with Normandy (Also paving the way for Bishop Roger Clinton). The French language dominated both high society and the Church (including music, literature and architecture this was a great disaster for Englishmen or for some a turning point in English culture.

# DOOMSDAY BOOK

William compiled the famous Doomsday Book, which accompanied a massive expansion of record keeping, never before known in England. Doomsday was a survey of every manor, every village, every wood, every hill and every feudal holding and worker King William could tax. By 1080 the King knew exactly what he owned; how much land was out to tenure, and what it was worth.

Normans purged their sins by endowing Monasteries and Priories, generously endowing houses, land, titles and chattels for their upkeep. In 1125, for example Jeoffrey de Clinton endowed Kenilworth Abbey/Priory in Warwickshire for Augustinian Canons. Bretford Priory followed in 1154 for Benedictine Nuns. In 1336 Sir William de Clinton endowed Maxstock Priory, Warwickshire for Augustinian Canons. Rayner the Flemming endowed Kirklees Priory.

Before the Conquest the Lords of the Manor were English. after the Conquest the Lords of the Manors were Normans Flemish or Breton, living in a wooden fort on top of a mound, speaking French, which few of his Saxon villeins understood.

The villein workers were desperately poor, had no rights whatsoever, and were unable to leave the manor. Nevertheless they were secure in their misery and always had food. A villein held about an acre of land in return, he worked much of the week for the Lord of the Manor.

# The Death of William the Conqueror

In July 1087, soldiers from the French Fort of Mantes raided into Normandy. William retaliated and sacked the Fort in July 1087, but received an injury from which he died. His body was carried to his church of St Stephens at Caen.

# The Clintons Rise and Rise

His eldest son Robert succeeded to Normandy. His youngest son, William Rufus became King of England. Norman French domination of England continues for centuries. All the while the Clintons were marrying into the English aristocracy to become Earls, Barons, Lords, Admirals and being summoned to Parliament.

THE CLINTONS RISE & RISE

ENGLAND'S HEADINGHAM CASTLE, ESSEX.
AN ORIGINAL NORMAN KEEP

THE JOUST MASTER
OF CEREMONIES

BATTLE KNIGHTS AT A
HEADINGHAM RE-ENACTMENT

BATTLE KNIGHTS AT A HEADINGHAM RE-ENACTMENT

LAYER MARNEY TOWERS, ESSEX. BUILT ON THE SITE OF A NORMAN KEEP OVERLOOKING THE RIVER BLACKWATER. OPEN TO TOURISTS AT SET TIMES DURING THE SPRING AND SUMMER.

THE BEST OF EUROPE'S KNIGHTS
FLOCK TO DUKE WILLIAM'S CAUSE.

THE BEST OF EUROPE'S KNIGHTS
FLOCK TO DUKE WILLIAM'S CAUSE.

# THE AUTHOR'S NOTES ON 50 YEARS OF RELIGIOUS STUDY

## STOP BLAMING GOD

In the late 1960's, I spent six months working with a wonderfully talented and great man in every respect, whose job it was to produce and direct mounted outside broadcast programmes for the Sunday Services on T.V.

Having trained and worked in almost every job in a television studio and outside broadcast unit, there was not much I did not know about making a television programme. What the job did afford me was the opportunity to enjoy long discussions with some quite senior clergy in both the Catholic Church and Church of England, during the drives to the various venues.

One question that always came under discussion, and continues to arise on both T.V. and radio even 45 years later is this; "how do I explain to my flock why God did not prevent this flood, or that storm, or the disaster that has ruined livelihoods and lives in my Diocese?"

The answer was and remains simple. Tell your congregation to stop blaming God. God has nothing to do with these disasters.

Planet Earth is a living, independent entity. It has a tectonic plate system that by subduction, moves great continents under each other about one millimetre per year. This live, moving system alone is responsible for volcanic eruptions, earthquakes and tsunamis. Planet Earth also has a giant weather system that ranges across the whole plant. The temperatures of Earth's oceans affect weather patterns around the globe. Then there are the ice ages followed by the melting of the ice ages, fetching the coming of the very warm periods in Earth's history.

All these systems are connected in ways that are not yet fully understood by scientists. All these systems march onwards every minute of every day doing their own thing. The Earth and its complex Earth systems have their own existence completely independent of man.

If man chooses to live on a fault line within an Earth quake zone, or a flood plan, or near rivers that flood, or close to the shore line in and around Indonesia, where catastrophic events will happen. What has that to do with God?

Almighty God does not cause or bring about these disasters; they happen because that is how our planet works.

Man pays little or no regard to living in dangerous areas, and to prove the point, when there is an earthquake, flood or any other Earth made disaster, man will be quick to rebuild his residence and life on the same spot that the disaster took place. Man will even build suburbia where disaster has taken place.

God, or The Powers of The Universe exist completely outside the physical structure of this planet. So please stop making excuses for, or blaming God for every disaster. God has absolutely nothing to do with them.

Yes, We can still pray to God for a miracle, but such prayers would be for a miracle of healing for example, and this miracle can happen. However, this is a completely different topic for a different book.

The secret writings in the ancient scrolls uncovered by Templar Knights in Jerusalem reveal information about the doctrine of the early church which give a story that is quite different to that which has come down to us today. It is easy to understand therefore, why leading churches of that time were incensed by and even afraid of their manuscripts , and wanted them seized and destroyed before their contents became public knowledge. Indeed any religious institution that claim to this day that both access to God and salvation was only available through their priests, does not want a different truth to arrive in the public domain, even today.

An early scroll states that Mary and Joseph had sons and a daughter, the eldest of whom were Jesus and James; all brought up to be teachers of Righteousness in a strict secretarian movement, where the teachers were celibate, did not eat meat, or drink strong drink, and did not cut their hair. Their teachings were, that those who followed the way could achieve illumination quite independently of the intervention of a third party from any organized religion. That is to say there is no necessity for a mediator between an individual and God. Not a doctrine that the early church wanted to escape into the public arena. Churches kept control over their congregations by insisting that no individual had access to God but by them.

## POLITICS TO EXCLUDE WOMEN FROM THE CHURCH AS PRIESTS AND TEACHERS

Mary Magdalene was from Magdala, a village close to the sea in Galilee, a supporter and teacher in the villages of Galilee. A favourite of Jesus and prominent in all the Gospels. The first of the Disciples to see the resurrected Christ after the crucifixion. Mary Magdalene undoubtedly established an undisputed precedent for women priests in the church. The church in Rome decided for political reasons to exclude women from the possibility of becoming priests. The church leaders took steps of excluding Mary Magdalene from biblical texts that described her as a Disciple and Teacher, tagging her instead as a prostitute, also ordering that all texts including apocryphal gospels referring to Mary Magdalene as a Disciple and Teacher to be brought up to the church and destroyed.

This solution was to bring forward Holy Mary mother of Jesus to be the intermediary between God and man. Time has shown this revelation by the church to be a miracle, and no one in the right mind would want to change the important role of our Holy Mary in the church today.

## INDISPUTABLE PRECEDENTS FOR WOMEN PRIESTS AND BISHOPS

It was a deception and sin for the early church in Rome to destroy most of the written evidential truth about the role Mary Magdalene played in the early church, because catholic priests did not want to serve alongside women. Their action was a sin and evil because they tried to destroy an indisputable precedent for women to play a leading role as priest of the church. Mary Magdalene was a teacher in Galilee, and a favourite of Christ. Who then, on Gods earth has the right to take away this precedent that depriving women from serving as Priests in the church for 2000 years. Whatever the politics of the church, a lie is a lie, and the truth is the truth. No one; priest or layperson that does not understand this eternal truth will ever reach genuine illumination. Truth and goodness are entangled in time and will always, yes always emerge again over time to be shouted from the highest rooftops.

## MORE POLITICS ABOUT JAMES THE BROTHER OF JESUS

In the third and fourth centuries the church in Rome developed that most beautiful story of stories, a miracle to this day - The Virgin Birth in Bethlehem. Similar to the story of the Moon Goddess. What church leaders began to fear at that time was the emergence of several independent and reliable scrolls uncovered by Knights Templar in the Holy Lands, attesting to the importance of James, the brother of Jesus, being appointed by Jesus to head the church in Jerusalem after his death, which James did for thirty years.

Rome ordered biblical scholars to buy up and destroy any scrolls of text written about James. Biblical scribes were also ordered to write James out from biblical texts, or at least to describe him in a way to cast doubt on his authenticity.

The Reason for this panic was the uncertainty that the fact that Jesus had a brother might cast on Rome's own story of the Virgin Birth. In the end the church was again unsuccessful, because the truth yet again entangled in time re-emerged 2000 years later in the independent 'Dead Sea Scrolls' the publication of which the church managed to suppress for 50 years. For the eventual release of the scrolls we have to thank the brilliant Professor Robert Eisemann pre-eminent biblical scholar.

Manuscripts from independent sources in the countries close to Palestine, reveal that secret knowledge was imparted by Jesus and his brothers James and John, to their original disciples, but only a few were able to unlock those secrets. No way was found to effectively impart this sacred knowledge to large numbers or large groups, although they tried. The sacred knowledge instructed the Teachers and Disciples of the Church to remain celibate, eat no animal, drink no strong drink, to practice meditation and healing, and gain illumination by tapping into all the knowledge that ever was and ever will be.

## THANK YOU TO RE-ENACTMENT GROUPS

We wish to thank all the numerous members of the re-enactment groups and invididuals in those groups who posed for our camera and gave us encouragement to use the resulting photographs in this book.

## PRAISE & THANKS FOR ESSEX COUNTY COUNCIL

Thank you to Essex County Council for their success in restoring and maintaining important historic sites and the undoubted benefits to adults and children visiting those sites where they see history come alive.

## THANKS TO SUNDAY TIMES & DAILY EXPRESS

For permission to use the Sunday Times articles and Daily Express photograph of Emily Roddham, English ancestral cousin to Hillary Clinton.

Our thanks to Tate Modern.